Living with and Loving ADHD and Neurodivergency

By

Sylvia Clare

and

David Hughes

Copyright Sylvia Clare and David Hughes

ISBN 978-1-7393234-3-1

No part of this book may be reproduced or stored in a retrieval system, or transmitted in any form or by any means electronic, mechanical, photocopying, recording, or otherwise, without express permission by the publishers and/or authors.

Cover design by David Hughes *(any similarities between the authors and the cartoon characters are intentional).*

Published by Clarity Books
first published in 2019
Second edition 2021
Third edition 2024

Clarity books c/o sylvia.clare@btinternet.com

Royalties

Fifty percent of all royalties go to

Anti-Slavery International is the only UK-based charity exclusively working to eliminate all forms of slavery throughout the world by investigating and exposing current cases of slavery, campaigning for its eradication, supporting the initiatives of local organisations to secure the freedom of those in slavery or vulnerable to it, and pressing for more effective implementation of national and international laws against slavery. Founded in 1839 by British abolitionists, it is the world's oldest international human rights organisation.

Also by the Authors

Non-fiction

Raising the Successful Child

Trust Your Intuition - illustration by David Hughes

Who Will I Become

Living the Life You Want

The Well-Mannered Penis - illustrations by David Hughes

No Visible Injuries – a Memoir

Travelling the World – Emotionally

Travelling the world Spiritually

The Buddha House – a memoir

Poetry by Sylvia Clare
The Musicians Muse, Black and White, Love and Chocolate, Gaia's Angry Daughter

Fiction

Julia - a murder mystery based on the Isle of Wight, by David Hughes

The Honest Liar – a trans-generational trauma thriller, by David Hughes

Index

Introduction	7
Einstein's Theory of ADHD	8
1. What is ADHD	10
2. What causes ADHD	15
3. ADHD and common but undiscussed dimensions	19
4. ADHD and Mindfulness	29
5. Buddhism and my wife's ADHD	49
6. ADHD and time management	53
7. Living with ADHD	64
8. I have ADHD and am Highly Sensitive	72
9. How ADHD views Neurotypicals	80
10. Travelling with ADHD	91
11. Positive Qualities of ADHD	99
12. Confession Time	109
13. The Unintentional Cruelty of Normalcy	116
14. Repeat After Me	123
15. So You Want to be Friends?	128
16. The Joys of ADHD	136

17. Socialising	148
18. Living Well with ADHD	153
19. Living Well with Someone with ADHD	153
20. PTSD, ADHD and its complications	158
21. Sylvia Clare ADHD, PTSD	168
22. Loving Yourself with ADHD	174
23. Someone with ADHD	186
24. Enjoying Life after Diagnosis	191
25. ADHD Saved My Life - Possibly	196
26. Where do we go from here?	202
27. Monkey Mind – a poem	205
28. How do People with ADHD find their Futures?	208
Further reading	215

Introduction

We realised we both had a lot to say about ADHD and ND generally as a result of our very neurodiverse family, both its struggles and its joys. Understanding all our differences made it possible to accommodate and support each other in ways that we had not been able to do so before.

Our shared mindfulness practice also worked in our favour and was a hugely supportive influence into this process of finally working together and understanding each other as complex beings rather than wilfully difficult beings.

Many of the chapters in this book started off as stand alone essays until it gradually became clear there was a book in them, as a collection. So there may be some repetition of some ideas from one chapter to another, but they stand in their space as well.

Einstein's theory of ADHD

1. Black holes exist anywhere you happen to have left an object you need

2. There will never be enough space to accommodate the objects you wish to leave lying around

3. Time speeds up when you are late and slows when you have nothing to do

4. It is impossible to finish all of the things you start without bringing in someone else to finish some of them for or with you.

5. Diaries only work if you look in them and even then, the time between looking and acting upon them is directly proportional to fulfilling the task

6. When tidying up you will always notice other people's stuff before your own

7. If someone is waiting for you or has just served up a meal, you will always find something elsewhere that needs your attention.

8. Money expands to accommodate the things you want to do or buy

9. The ability to focus is directly proportional to the interest you have in a subject and the amount of effort it takes to achieve it

David Hughes

1. What is ADHD?

There's got to be a deep voice within you that is untouched by definitions. And it is there that you become divinely who you are. Viola Davis

ADHD is a recognised cognitive disability based on two main deficiencies, inattentiveness and hyperactivity. It is so much more than that of course but these are the two main foci of attention, seen as deficits and problems for others, especially as behavioural and educational difficulties in childhood.

ADHD makes everything in modern / western life more difficult on a basic or functional level, not just a little bit more but seriously challenging in some cases. Except that you think this level of challenge is normal because that is all you have known. And then you just believe you are a failure at life, until you realise it is the other way round. It can be traumatic, exhausting, undermining, a destroyer of self-esteem and self-worth, a creator of needless frustration with yourself and the basis of emotional self-abuse.

School makes it so much worse. It did for myself and my two sons at least, and my husband was pretty traumatised by school too. When I worked as a school counsellor, in the early 2000's, not enough had changed even then. School is not designed for people who are different and is thus abusive by default, unintentionally, but definitely, wasting more potential than can ever be measured.

Neurotypical people can learn as much from ND so an integrated school which can adapt is the answer. Segregation might make it easier in the short term but how about fitting in with society later on. We all need to learn how to relate to each other openly and with kindness.

1. Education regimes for people with ADHD should roughly speaking include the following: a lot of movement, especially forms with self-expression e.g. dance, drama, yoga, athletics, swimming, running, definitely martial arts, and perhaps team games although I found them impossible due to the social pressures and the emotional traumas of competition. Anything that burns off the excess energy that keeps us feeling driven. Let the child choose their own outlet though - don't impose on

someone who doesn't feel safe or confident to tackle an activity. ND children are very unique and individuals may love one thing and another child be terrified of the same thing

2. Then we should be allowed to find our own focus. For instance, I adore reading and once I had climbed a few trees to release excess energy, I would get lost in books forever at weekends. Give me a good historical novel and I will still absorb all the facts, but a history textbook will send me to sleep. A well-researched historical novel can do it all for me. Same with cross-cultural literature and poetry. I can get more geography out of a good travel memoir with factual information embedded and philosophy and psychology positively jump out of well-written fiction. Maths made sense when it was to do with nature, gardening, or wildlife. I could go on, but this would have worked well for me.

3. And let me/us work at my own pace. School was painfully slow for me, and totally disjointed in the way it was broken up into subject slots. Some might need a slower pace. I could have completed a year's syllabus on history in just a few days if the historical novels were good enough and after I had run off the

excess energy. Instead, I spent endless hours tirelessly picking the paint off the flaking radiators to try and calm myself down, these were some of my earliest mindfulness experiences – or possibly OCD. Being focused on something simple and in the present moment was what I needed. The school caretakers weren't too pleased though.

For other children with ADHD it might be something else. Art for instance would have been great for my sons and they could have gone on into all sorts of creative careers. School killed art for them both too. I was told I had no artistic talent, and it turns out I also have dysgraphia so cannot draw or handwrite legibly either.

Other topics include woodcraft and gardening, and any outdoor activities, woodcraft and nature studies. You can teach an awful lot of core curriculum topics with these activities. If they are interested in dinosaurs, let them take that as far as they can. Someone needs to become a palaeontologist after all. Use the focusing skills we do have productively and let them develop in their own way. We are each individual, but this way of teaching can be done across ages and topics. It is roughly how Steiner schools work and also how John Dewey suggested it would be a better education for all children. It is not rocket science to say that changing the educational approach for children with ADHD is better than medicating and undermining their potential.

2. What causes ADHD?

As far as I know it is still open to debate.

Possibly is it caused by dopamine deficiencies in the brain

Possibly it is caused by too many theta waves being produced by the brain

Possibly it is a throwback to early man needing to be more widely alert and less narrowly focused except when necessary i.e when hunting, though neanderthal humans show remarkable levels of cultural development and most of us nowadays have a percentage of neanderthal DNA so ADHD is not a throwback gene deficiency

Possibly it is a result of early trauma (nurture) since many of the symptoms of long-term trauma overlap with ADHD and other forms of neurodivergency(ND)

Possibly it is caused by genetic inheritance (nature), as it certainly runs in families in one form or another, but that could also be transgenerational trauma affecting genetic patterns and manifesting as neurodivergency(ND) in one form or another

Possibly it is a little bit of all of these and that is why science still cannot pin it down completely.

Nature/nurture influences are known to interact and cannot be separated out from each other easily, even with identical twin studies. There are little switches (called alleles) on genes that can get turned on and off to all sorts of stimuli and with all sorts of outcomes. Genetics is extraordinarily complicated, so I do not want to oversimplify anything.

The more deeply science burrows into genetics, the more apparent it is that simplistic divisions of this gene or that influence are removed and a deeply complex interaction between many genes and many influences is the true picture.

Whatever it is and wherever it comes from, it is very real and a struggle for those who live with it. But it could be less so. It is not a discipline or an obedience issue. That is imposed from those who would have us other than as we are, who lack the flexibility to work creatively with children, and to embrace all deviations from narrow norms.

ADHD is not a discipline issue ever! ND is not bad behaviour – it is our best expression of where we are and what is going on in our bodies. Actually, in children, this applies to neurotypical (NT) children too, but that is a different discussion.

Having said that, I hope this book will help you to consider its merits too.

There are always gifts in all things in life if you look for them and that is what we have done in our own lives. That is my whole approach to living well. Mindfulness taught me that. It is the path of self-acceptance and enjoying life in our own ways.

Does science need to know in the end? Do we need a diagnostic certainty? Answer that yourself when you have finished reading this book.

Is ADHD only possible in children?

It may appear to lessen in adulthood because of learned strategies for managing, and masking (pretending you're not ND by suppressing your expressions). Everyone can achieve this, ADHD or no ADHD. Life is always work in progress, and I am still struggling to live with it, as you will read. But that can be said of everyone anyway!

Is it a disability?

Yes, but not for the reason you would think! It certainly needs disability status at the moment, for the legal protections that offers us from those who would abuse us out of ignorance. The Disability Equality Act states that allowances must be made for ND so that we have the same opportunities and chances as NT people.

Emotional consequences

My own life has gone through several partial or near complete collapses, most of it originating from my ADHD or PTSD issues. I have learned to be resilient, yet I am so sensitive and vulnerable in my core. I think this may be true of many people with ADHD. It has been a journey of hard won discovery and great happiness. ADHD has a been a huge struggle and yet a great teacher. I think it has made me a better person.

3. ADHD and common but undiscussed dimensions

The problem is not the problem. The problem is your attitude to the problem.

Captain Jack Sparrow

Most people think ADHD is just a 'problem', with hyperactivity and inattention as its principle deficiencies. Indeed its title suggests this is all there is to know about it. Yet it is so much more.

Medically, ADHD is characterised by specific behaviours which can be measured. This enables diagnosticians and clinicians and also drug companies to identify along those criteria.

Unfortunately this limited view and understanding of ADHD diagnostically means that many aspects of ADHD are ignored because they cannot be quantified, and yet they are very much part of the experience of having ADHD. This defines who will or will not be diagnosed with ADHD and also who gets treatment and into programmes or who does not.

The point about ADHD is that we are not the same, we are all individuals so not all applies to everyone, but much of it will. It is a spectrum disorder. A spectrum disorder is like a long buffet table with lots of options to pick from. If you only manifest one or two options you do not qualify, no matter how challenging these issues are. If half the buffet is missing then your options are ignored, rather like being a vegan and a meat eaters meal. So you won't count either. What you need is a tick on your plate for enough often options to qualify as a diagnostic syndrome. Many females do not exhibit external restlessness. It is on the inside instead, and thus they do not have ADHD. But they do! This is being more understood but still half the buffet is missing. That has not been rectified, though the level of comorbidity means that many ND diagnoses are now merging, such as AUDHD - autism and ADHD. Things are evolving and we are being listened to more nowadays on a diagnostic level, just not on the social front

Emotional dysregulation probably causes the greatest amount of distress and yet it is totally overlooked. We think and approach our life management skills in totally different ways to neurotypicals. We tend to lead very intense and passionate lives with high highs and lower lows than others. We are not Bi-Polar, we are just different emotionally, though some are diagnosed co-morbid with Bi-polar. This comes from a tendency to medicalise all alternative ways of being human. We have the same types of emotions, but just more intensely, and struggle with how we can express this, or not. We often get overwhelmed by our emotional intensity, and it can cause difficulties if not understood.

Other problems include sleep difficulties and relationship conflicts which arise from this intensity.

If we are angry then we are deeply angry, but it may also dissipate quickly if something else comes along, and we tend not to hold grudges.

If we love, then we love deeply and passionately and so on.

If we are hurt by the attitudes, judgements and criticisms of other's, we are used to it and have built up some resilience and even expectation to it unless we are also highly sensitive (HSP) in which case we experience great unhappiness and sometimes physical pain from the energy of those attitudes and judgments, which can then lead to self-harming, addictions, and other forms of expressions of that hurt. However many people with ADHD do struggle with feelings of self-worth, mostly being in the negative and based on constant negative feedback that has been repeatedly swallowed and kept hidden deep inside. This can create anxiety which exacerbates the more negative ADHD symptoms and traits.

Sleep difficulties

If your nervous system is continuously overloaded by life, then it is hardly any surprise that sleep difficulties occur. My eldest son had terrible sleep deprivation as a young child, but I was told he just didn't need that much sleep, not that there was something wrong that stopped him from sleeping and therefore me too. I was an exhausted mother with a son whose body wouldn't let him sleep, and we now know that this can lead to a developmental lowering of intelligence and brain development and all sorts of health issues later on in life. Nowadays he can sleep pretty deeply but I think those early days had a negative impact on him in many ways, though I am not sure what we could have done about it other than drug him into sleep, which is not healthy sleep. I on the other hand have developed increasingly sporadic sleep and I can tell that even if I don't feel tired, it is more difficult to manage my ADHD symptoms when I am sleep reduced. The more sleep I can get the better, the less distracted and emotionally dysregulated I am and the better I can focus and concentrate.

Attention and focus issues

About 85% of our brain is involved with inhibitory behaviours, i.e. stopping behaviours, which are mostly subconscious. This is a protective / defensive adaptation of the human brain. The corpus striatum is the main area functioning on this level. It is a cluster of neurons in the base of the forebrain and is involved in

- cognition, mental awareness of motor and action planning,
- decision making,
- motivation, reinforcement/ learning from experience,
- reward perception.

Inhibitions enable us to focus on what matters in life. ADHDers have problems with selecting what to attend to because we have lower active inhibitors. We are constantly bombarded with inputs and there is no apparent filter in place to make it easier to manage this overload. In this way we are similar to autism, or ASD, which is often comorbidly diagnosed. It is also linked with Dyslexia, dyspraxia, dysgraphia, and dyscalculia. These are all ways in which the wiring of the brain makes it harder for certain people to function in a world which depends on very linear narrow approaches to writing, maths, drawing and other limited use of our incredible human brain capacity.

I used to think of all this as being very sad, as a disability, until I learned to look at it differently. Many of the additional differences are discussed in the next chapter on mindfulness and how it helped me.

Managing impulsivity

This is indeed such a conundrum to manage and that management comes in stages. The first stage is to recognise how, when and what the impulsivity manifests over - it is not all the time, so what does it react to - what are the catalysts for it. This takes some self-study and awareness but once you have got a picture of how your impulsivity affects you and what triggers it as well, you can start to recognise the patterns. I practice and teach mindfulness for ADHD so this is a very mindful approach but it works more or less.

If you forget to notice and act impulsively anyway, don't punish yourself for it but take a deep breath and start again - guilt, blame, and shame are very devastating for people with ADHD and from experience, make it far worse than it previously was, exacerbating the cycle of struggle and failure.

Reward yourself every time you do manage to stop yourself from being too impulsive, even if you stop yourself halfway through. Start to fine-tune your self-awareness about when it occurs and when it doesn't. It is more likely when you're more tired or have not done some physical workout to burn off the excess energy, which then leaps into another stimulus mode, impulsivity.

If these are your low ebb points, then be more aware of the risks at these times and find ways to manage them to get yourself through them more effectively. When I am suppressing an impulse to do something mad, I just jump up and down on the spot. My husband calls me his bouncy bouncy wife in his bouncy bouncy life, so it becomes fun instead of a problem.

Sometimes in the middle of a meal I just have to get up and jump for a few minutes - I am nearly 69 now and this still works for me. We just accept it as how life is and not bad manners. I can usually cope if we are out in public but actually prefer not to do that too often. Play around with this approach and see if it is workable for you over time - it has really helped both of us enormously and with both my sons too. It can be fun at family meal times lol!! I also sometimes hug them all with such enthusiasm and love that I also have to jump up and down at the same time. This is nicknamed Pogo Love and I ended up writing a poem about it for fun.

Pogo love

Sometimes the thrill of loving you
is just far too much for my frame to contain
and exuberance at life becomes overwhelming.

In those moments I must just stand
behind you, place my hands on your shoulders
and jump.

Up and down, for as long as it takes.
It doesn't matter that we are getting older now
or that my feet and ankles lack the vigour they once held.

It doesn't matter if you are standing drinking a cup of tea
Or contemplating the world in general.
I must place a hand on each shoulder and jump

for joy, for the sheer beauty of having you in my life.
I must jump until my energy ebbs enough
to settle down once more.

I must jump until I feel able to rest quietly
in that same space of love and appreciation.
I must jump until the surges of exuberance and emotion

are expressed in their fullness, their passion, their happiness.
I must jump until you stop me and hold me and give me
a hug that lets me know you will hold me forever.

I may have white hair, and creaky bones, a spine that is slowly
collapsing
under the burdens life has piled upon it. Love throws that all off.
Love is youthful, full of energy, full of bounce.

And so I must jump. What can be better than pogo love?

Boing boing boing boing boing boing xxxxx

4. ADHD and Mindfulness

'Maybe the fear is that we are less than we think we are when the actuality is that we are much much more.' **Jon Kabat Zinn**

In 2016, at a Thich Nhat Hanh community (COI) family Mindfulness retreat in Stourbridge UK, I worked with families with Attention Deficit Hyperactivity Disorder (ADHD) diagnoses and I wanted to share some reflections on mindfulness practice and how it relates to ADHD. I believe this is important at this present time because more and more people are being diagnosed with ADHD and being medicated away from who they are. Mindfulness offers all people affected both directly or indirectly an opportunity to find a realistic and long-term response to this.

ADHD makes life difficult for adults and children alike. Being a spectrum condition, like autism, many people may have some ADHD tendencies but not the full-blown condition. In someone who has ADHD the brain is wired differently and just because such people behave differently, they are not being difficult, rude or thoughtless; ADHD does not imply an IQ deficit, one can still be highly intelligent with severe ADHD. We often are in fact, and also rather funny too. Many comedians are ADHD. Whether you are living with someone who has ADHD symptoms or are the diagnosed individual, or just perhaps likely to run up against someone with ADHD in your general life, (which is possibly most of us), this book may help you.

Not a developmental condition

One doesn't grow out of it, but rather develops survival strategies. My sons and I were all diagnosed with ADHD in adulthood. Mindfulness and meditation practice became hugely influential and beneficial. It offered realisable and realistic, but not easy solutions.

I realise that many people struggle when taking up the practice of mindfulness, but it is even more challenging for someone with ADHD and they do have to be highly motivated to achieve this. I started my own practice about 20 years before diagnosis, in my late 30's, and just found mindfulness and the Buddhist approach to life made sense of my struggles, all of them, not just the ADHD which at that time I did not even know about. I just thought I was weird. I was generally ok with that except when it seemed to sabotage my life again and again. For me there were many other factors involved too. I also got diagnosed with more or less life-long Complex trauma and PTSD (post-traumatic stress disorder) resulting from my traumatic childhood, from parents who perhaps did not know how to control or manage a child with ADHD without recourse to increasing levels of 'punishment', and who had their own mental health issues. But once I learned to manage the PTSD, the ADHD was still there, as it apparently had always been.

Neuroplasticity
Mindfulness has been shown to re-wire the brain over time (David Austin, Sarah Lazar, Richard Davidson etc.) The interesting question is: can the brain be rewired where there are structural deficits such as those in ADHD. The answer researched thus far is probably yes, some of them at least, with many iterations and great effort. But there are limitations to this too, as more recent research by Sonuga-Barke et al. has shown. To understand how, one has to understand a little more about how ADHD manifests.
There are many features of ADHD which I shall address in turn to demonstrate how this mindfulness approach can work to

ameliorate the additional difficulties and challenges that ADHD can present.

Impulsivity.

This is an ADHD spectrum behaviour sometimes leading to serious social and legal problems, but nearly always causing problems especially in childhood being seen as a discipline issue. Doing things and saying things without awareness of likely repercussions and implications. I call it my blurtyness as I tend to be too honest and well intentioned in speaking my mind when it may not be helpful or wanted. That doesn't mean I am wrong, just that socially it is rather unusual.

Social consequences are just not on the ADHD radar and take a massive effort to understand and recognise. Impulsivity can also be part of their charm and strength, being spontaneous and generous, fun, lively and generally quite innovative, often being prepared to go where others are far too timid.

The very nature of impulsivity can be challenging and I have found this offers good opportunities to practice, i.e. don't allow annoyance at superficial behaviours but look deeply into the intention behind it, which is often positively motivated.

Mindfulness helps develop awareness of physical tensions and other symptoms of impulsivity and allow one to step in on one's own body. It takes time for anybody to learn this skill but can really make a difference to the social competence and confidence of someone with ADHD. I am now aware of consequences most of the time and my son is gradually learning about them although still struggles to recognise what they might be and when they might arise.

I found also the teaching on Karma and especially Thay's (Thich Nhat Hanh's) teaching of Inter-being really helped to make more sense of it all and enabled me to forgive my errors, and those of others, by recognising how important the motivation factor really is. What you do is far less important than why you do it. Someone with ADHD might not know this. They often do not have any access to the motivation behind their behaviours, it just comes as an impulse. How much responsibility can we attribute on this basis? Learning to stop for a moment, as often as possible, just allows you an insight into that motivation and (MAY??) allow you to make a choice rather than react, but with ADHD it is much harder.

Empathy and the rules of social relationships

Empathy and the rules of social relationships are rarely understood by people with ADHD in terms of both impacts on the person with ADHD themselves, and on those with whom they come into contact. Similarly to autism, ADHD often means being overwhelmed by crowds and struggling to understand and cope with social cues; these skills have to be learned.

Often people with ADHD are forthright and literal, childlike, naive, rarely with malice intended. Their honesty and openness can be refreshing in contrast to some social rules which include various forms of dishonesty. You know where you stand and you can decide to go with it or to be offended - your choice. However they can also be quite devious as a coping mechanism to deal with what they might feel as their failures or abnormalities, and as an avoidance of the endless critical attitudes that come from other people.

Mindful awareness and self-acceptance makes this all more manageable for both those with and those without but who are living with or relating to someone with ADHD, and helps to drop the need for negative survival skills like deviousness.

Concentration

The most prominent feature of ADHD is also the most commonly understood challenge, that of very fragmented concentration on every-day things and, most of all, the educational sphere, hence the policy to drug diagnosed children into submission.

But what is less well known is that the opposite is also true. Most people with ADHD can hyper-focus on things that grab their attention, and I mean really absorb and focus with an intensity that can appear obsessive. This has been the most successful role of mindfulness in my own life and what also eventually drew my son into the practice. Once you can recognise how much mindfulness will alleviate the problems of living with ADHD, it becomes an absolute must do approach to life. Once I recognised that for myself, and it had to be my own discovery, no one could have told me, it became something I was able to work with eagerly. After all, mindfulness is the gradual development of focussed attention, but someone with ADHD will need many, many more iterations before it starts to have an effect. I always come back to the teaching of the student and the master to help keep mé encouraged.

'Master, master, my meditation practice is terrible, my attention is everywhere and I cannot sit still at all.'
'This will pass' says the master quietly.
A week later the student comes and says 'oh master you are so wise, now my meditation practice is so calm and I can sit still and peacefully through all the sessions'.
'This will pass' says the master quietly.
This simple teaching helped me to come through the struggles of sitting and being restless and unfocussed and helped me to relax with my own experience of sitting practice, however that is and on any given day. It is not a competition, it is a goalless state, and ADHD might make it harder on one level but once you appreciate the goalless part of it you can be with it wholeheartedly, whatever arises.
As Thich Nhat Hanh says 'enjoy your practice'. I do not enjoy my sitting practice, but I have learned how to make the most of it and enjoyment has grown from that and exploring all the other ways in which one can develop a mindfulness practice. Now I love it.

Criticism resilience

People with ADHD have to be resilient to criticism and rejection; they attract lots. Mindful approaches to life make criticism less painful because you can convert criticism into useful feedback and learn how to recognise when the criticism is valid and when it is someone else's problem with judgements, i.e. their projection onto you of their own personal agendas. It can be very helpful to understand why other people's judgements may not be valid. They do not know or understand you fully.

ND people often experience acute rejection dysphoria. This is an issue to explore through mindfulness too – it helped me.

Delay aversion

This is more than not being able to wait for things to happen or to arrive, it becomes physical distress. Tests show clear preferences to take lesser rewards than face delay, even if delay means receiving more. The smaller reward is less challenging or disappointing than the distress and struggle to wait and be patient. It is not greed or snatching but seeking to avoid the tension created by waiting. Self-awareness arises from the practice of mindfulness and studying Thay's interpretations of

Buddha's teachings in depth for their psychological content. This really helped me to understand how to challenge my own sense of permanent urgency and to use that as a place of relaxation, to notice when that kind of impulse was taking me over, to step back and breathe. It doesn't mean it has all gone of course, far from it, but that I can work with it positively.

Hyperactivity

The hyperactivity part of ADHD, the need to keep moving, is a particular challenge of social expectations for children, even more for the managing adults, creating the illusion of a badly controlled, naughty child. They are not. The physical backlash of suppressing the impetus to keep moving can be difficult to understand, the need to release the suppressed tension in the body can feel quite desperate and almost violent. My son when he started school aged nearly five, was told to sit down and he did. But then he got up again. This happened often and he was then shouted at regularly by his reception teacher, often right near his ear. He had repetitive glue ear and perforated ear drums and this teacher often caused him considerable pain. I went to see her and she said she didn't care as she was retiring at the end of the year. I regret not having followed that up more fully at the time but I was also struggling then and didn't know how to. That teacher made my five yr. old son feel traumatised, fearful and overwhelmed by the negativity of school. He asked if he could leave school within two terms of being there. I had no capacity to facilitate this so he had to stay there and be unhappy, at five yrs old.

Learning to work with the physical tension and the breath has helped me enormously although there are still times when sitting still for meditation is impossible. I have learned to use micro-movements — tiny rocking movements that help me to release the tension of physical inactivity. However, I often find my body has just moved of its own accord and I've learned not to be afraid of other people being irritated by that but for them to see that as their own mindfulness practice challenge. I often need to remind myself that I must be self-compassionate and not judge myself for what I still have to face but rather to recognise how incredibly hard it has been to get this far. And often nowadays when I sit, I am transported to wherever it is we all go in deep meditation, it does happen with perseverance.

Positive experiences

My practice of mindfulness, in all its wonderful rich layers of teaching, has utterly transformed my experience of myself and the world around me so that it is ok to be me, to have ADHD qualities (not deficits- just differences) that can make me frustrating but also fun to be with, and to enjoy the present moments as they parade through. If I look back I can see the many skins I have shed on this journey and accept each one as part of that transition.

This can apply to everyone.

I can really enjoy my relationship with my son whose ADHD was once a massive and overwhelming challenge for me as a stressed out single parent. Both he and I have changed, grown and developed a deeper relationship and appreciation of each other as parent and adult son through this journey into the ADHD /mindful approach to life.

Emotional Hyper-arousal and Rejection Sensitivity

This is an extreme form of emotional sensitivity which literally has people in tears for so many mis-understandings. The rejection dimension I suspect comes from so much rejection and criticism based on other symptoms and creates a hypersensitivity in some people who also have a hypersensitive emotional network. Often people with and forms of ND just cannot suppress their emotions and indeed it would not be healthy for them to do this. It is probably the basis for my own PTSD during childhood, being punished so severely for something I could not control and being a very sensitive person as I also am. My own development of a mindfulness practice has enabled me to recognise when I am being oversensitive and mostly, but not always, be able to manage those reactions reasonably enough. The self-observation skills that mindfulness develops in us really helps to recognise that our own hypersensitivity may not be the real story — but nevertheless I am still very prone to those feelings. I can manage them positively nowadays too, which helps enormously, because the reactive dimension to this can backfire on me and does require those close to me to be very tolerant and understanding at times.

How mindfulness helps so much.
The challenges of ND are definitely assisted by mindfulness. Can you sit? Can you concentrate your mind at all or even start to slow it down? Can you learn to eat more slowly? Well yes

you can but perhaps not as far or as quickly as someone who does not have ND.

So don't be hard on yourself if you struggle to eat slowly, and still finish first.

And don't accept the judgements of those who think they are better at their practice because they have eaten their meal more slowly.

They have missed the point of mindfulness if they view you in this way.

Accept that what you can achieve is good enough and will, like everyone else's practice, improve over time, but perhaps at different rates.

Another very powerful teaching comes to mind here which really helped me; that the form is not the thing itself, that having the external appearance of good mindfulness skills and intellectual understanding are not being mindful, they can in fact be very controlled and ego originated indeed. It is what comes from the heart that matters; the love of the practice, of this approach to life, of yourself exactly as you are, whilst knowing that this self is not fixed but will evolve over time, that is how I feel the dharma inside my own heart. I have met with many NT's who have a good external appearance of mindfulness but it is more ego acting than heart commitment and that is not true mindfulness at all. ThichNhat Hanh even talks about this in his monastics in his translation of the Diamond Sutra. Do not judge by external appearances, it is the motivation, the heart that really matters.

Watching the breath

Was this ever going to be a tough one for me? But watching the breath gets easier with determination, you cannot get a person with ADHD to concentrate unless you really grab their attention, then they will hyper-focus on learning and understanding everything they can about the practice. So it has got to come with bells on in the first place or else offer them something they really want for themselves. The latter came for me as I had struggled so much everywhere for my whole life, and believed myself a completely useless failure. It gave me hope and I hyper-focussed for over two decades on the teachings of Thich Nhat Hanh and other Buddhist or mindfulness teachers as they were presented to us. I still do in the right moments. But if not in the right moment, I can't force it. It has to be when I am ready and receptive, then I practice like nothing else exists (it doesn't, does it!).

What was a game changer for me though was that Thay said 'enjoy your practice, do it but enjoy it.' John Kabat Zinn had told me the opposite on a retreat some years earlier, 'You dont have to like it you just have to do it' - so mindfulness and sitting had become a form of self torture instead. For many John Kabat Zinn's approach works wonderfully so please don't take this as a criticism of his way of teaching, one's practice and what works is a very personal thing, Thich Nhat Hanh gave me permission to develop my own approach to a form of practice which worked for me, but also which worked for my brand of ADHD / PTSD. I am still pretty traditional but I have worked out how to make it fit me rather than follow instructions that don't help me at all and can even re-trigger my PTSD if I am not careful.

On the outside I can appear less than calm or slowing down, but there has been a vast transformation over time. Sitting continues to be my greatest challenge but now I accept and manage the need to move; sometimes I go really deeply and sometimes not, just like the rest of you.

Sometimes sitting is just endurance and I need to go for a fast walk or run afterwards to release the tension which builds up.

But on the right day I can hyper-focus on my breath and stay still for ages, and I can't plan which day it will be, ever.
My favourite meditations are active ones: walking, gardening and manual chores. I was extremely grateful to the sister at Lower Hamlet who taught us how to walk mindfully and quickly at the same time. I'd done that for years but believed it wrong, the best I could manage but not 'good enough'. Now I know I am doing my practice just like anyone else. I do also enjoy very slow mindful walking meditation practice when I am right for it. Right practice/ right time.

Finding what worked for me
This was a process of trial and experimentation. One approach was creating a mantra, or an affirmation, or a gatha, (a phrase one can repeat), out of the present moment. This kind of focus was a great way of learning to concentrate when I needed to, along the lines of 'this moment, this breath,' repeated endlessly as I walk, and in time to my steps, or to my planting or weeding or laundry.
The Plum Village tradition also offers songs based on mindful teachings and I can sing these silently inside my own head when I need to stop and re-focus. There are so many ways mindful

focus can be made more accessible for those with ADHD. Sometimes I just need to remind myself to be calm and take a single breath, and sometimes I need something stronger.
When my PTSD erupts I add to it with 'in this moment I am safe', 'in this moment all is well', and 'in this moment I am loved'.
Sometimes words more along the lines of impermanence (this too will pass) especially if I have been badly PTSD triggered, which at the point of writing still happens.

Non-Judgement

Non-judgement is one of the biggest challenges. We all judge without even realising it. Recognising the pervasive nature of my own self-judgement was very illuminating. Recognising how painful I find the judgement of others was another. Once I had unfrozen the PTSD it was so intensely painful that it physically hurt. Letting that go has resulted in reduced anxiety and the development of self-acceptance, a continual, iterative process. But I am now clear I will always have ADHD and I will always have to accept that what I can manage is enough.

Enjoy your mindfulness practice

One of Thay's most important teachings for me was that you should enjoy your practice but that you should also put effort into it. So John Kabat Zinn was also partially right. There are many ways of practicing mindfulness from the heart and the more orthodox disciplinarian approach will almost certainly not work for someone with ADHD. It is just too much of a struggle. I believe you can teach mindfulness to anyone with ADHD but first find a way to make it an important thing in their life. Don't judge how they practice; if it comes from the heart then it is good enough. The more physical forms of practice are almost certainly going to be easier to manage and enable you to feel that you are accomplishing something.

However don't give up on sitting either.

I found that starting with very short 'sits' helped me to realise the benefits and to make progress. I started with ten breaths. If I could manage that then I could manage eleven and so on. I no longer need to count. I also found that I do sometimes enjoy my sitting practice but mostly just struggle with my bodily need for movement as a counter stimulation, But I did start to notice how much better I felt if I did a short sit in the mornings and a few more very short ones during the day. This was more manageable in a busy life too, and more likely to be adhered to for me. Often I don't even sit, I just stop and stand for a few moments and breathe, stop and start again with a clear slate. If I forgot one then I could do the next one without any self-punishing thoughts, and I always noticed if I had missed a whole day, I just felt more jumbled inside than usual. Even if you don't know if someone has ADHD or not, but you find them a bit 'busy' in their practice, recognise that your judgements say more about your beliefs and expectations, your mental formations, than they do about the person you are judging, even if it is you.

I'm grateful for my ADHD. It makes me who I am, and I am greatly loved by my husband for exactly who I am. It took me many decades to feel like that though. For far too long I felt the outcast, useless etc. Now I know that cannot be true because of the understanding I have of Interbeing.

Let us celebrate ADHD through the practice of mindfulness, let us enjoy its wonderful positive qualities and help to re- educate a culture that sees it as a problem condition to be 'cured' by medication, when meditation and compassion is all that is really needed.

5. Buddhism and my wife's ADHD

'The mind is everything, what you think, you become.'
Buddhist teaching

I took up Buddhism when I was nineteen or so. Actually it was Hatha Yoga initially. I found this book written in the 1950's by a Doctor who had travelled to India to study Yoga that looked interesting and as I had just suffered a breakdown and needed something to bring me up from a low place, I thought maybe Yoga could help. This was in the day when Yoga was considered 'freaky', and if you weren't exploring any alternatives you had two prescription drugs, Valium and Librium, both of which made one feel detached but also remarkably foggy and dis-inclined to do anything, not my idea of living. So I started my practice and ditched them. From there I began to read about Buddhism and how the mind could change with practice and one could find peace of mind.

By the time I met Sylvia many years later I liked to think I was pretty sussed. I told her I didn't have any anger which she told me was the best ever chat up line. Imagine someone who had suffered Sylvia's childhood and early adulthood coming across someone who told her they were totally at peace with themselves! Of course this was not intended as a chat up line and I was not the cool dude I actually believed myself to be, but in my defence, who ever really sees their true self? So let's just say I was calm most of the time and that was enough for us to start with. We had this common interest in the mind, in 'spirituality', and she needed someone safe and I needed someone stimulating. A relationship made in heaven or perhaps in the self-help section of every bookshop at the time. Anyway we found something in each other that interested both of us. Sylvia talks about Mindfulness and its effect upon one, and Mindfulness is indeed part of the Noble Eightfold Path which as its name suggests is a list of eight suggested ways of living that will help one find peace of mind and live a better life. I think several of the eight ways are relevant to ADHD, for example Compassion, Right Motivation, Right Thought, Right Understanding to name a few. I don't believe there are any examples of the Buddha giving advice to someone with ADHD, mainly because it is a twentieth century diagnosis, but if he had, I imagine it would involve amongst other things telling them, to learn to understand their motivation when doing things, to have compassion for themselves, to practice Mindfulness, and to understand why others find it difficult to accept their differences and to practice Metta (loving kindness) for them.

I was brought up to be judgemental. It was an era of judgement coming not long after the Second World War, a black and white world of right and wrongs, of stereotyping, a world based on fear; fear of the Atomic bomb, fear of another war, fear of Communism and its polar opposite, Fascism.

The 1960's came and went with their open 'love everyone' approach but one's early influences remain and even though I had been following Buddhist principles for years when I met Sylvia, I know I judged people, and I initially judged her for the way she behaved. She confused me, leaving bookshops with seven or eight books when I was having difficulty spending on one. She seemed oblivious to the implications of her impulsive nature, (including taking up with me I might add). She was wonderfully 'out there' and yet everything in her life appeared to be on the edge of some potential disaster. I was a natural procrastinator, a man who assessed everything, who was frugal and in many ways quite boring. So her lifestyle was partly the attraction she held, but it was also scary! Why am I writing this? Because I want to explain that you can live with someone with ADHD even if you are a very staid, frugal and reasonably tidy person, you just need to loosen up and prepare for the ride! You never really know what will happen next and that is part of the fun.

6. ADHD and Time Management

'Oh dear, oh dear! I shall be too late.'

The White Rabbit – Alice in Wonderland

Did the White Rabbit have ADHD? We shall never know. ADHD is often linked with distractedness but not so often specifically about time issues.

I remember once my son was asked to make an appointment at a set time with a key worker. This is a seriously major achievement which would have taken some effort on his part. He got there on time and then he was asked to go away for ten minutes. He completely got distracted and went back half an hour later, when he got sanctioned for his lateness. They supposedly knew about his ADHD but thought they could punish him out of it.
IT DOESN'T WORK LIKE THAT!!!!!!!
I spent much of my life so anxious about being late, I am nearly always early. The advantage this gives me - time to loosen the knots of anxiety in my stomach about being on time. I was addicted to checking my watch every few minutes and it was

only when I was able to stop wearing a watch and calm down that I realised how much this had dominated my life. I just took it for granted that life was like this for me so that I could fit in with others and not let them down. Though I do know that happened sometimes, it never occurred to me how much others also let me down and seriously sometimes. It was always me in the wrong. When I completely forgot – goodness knows how many people took offence at that even though I had probably done my very best not to, in ways they would never have understood.

ADHD is not a disorder of knowing what to do, it's a disorder of doing what you know — at the right times and in the right places. Russell Barkley.

Planning tasks

If you want me or anyone with ADHD to do one thing immediately we will probably do it really well. I am really good at that kind of thing. But ask us to remember over time and it is a nightmare, our nightmare, recurring. I know this is true of both myself and my son, and many others.

Yesterday I had two tasks to complete, both short but sort of urgent. I knew the chances were that whichever one I did first the other one would be forgotten, and I was on my own at home. My tactic was to keep repeating the two tasks as a mantra until one was completed and I could then immediately get onto the second. I cannot trust myself to remember when I need to. I am always working double time to even keep on top of simple things. And this has always been the case, so not a product of my older years. But through mindful awareness I can manage this more effectively on my own. I have found ways to make it easier but only with mindfulness practice. If there had been more than two tasks though – who knows? I will just applaud myself for achieving two and remind myself that life doesn't end if you leave something for another day, it's just inconvenient, as long as it's just for me.

It doesn't matter how hard the activity is, the time management is far harder than anyone without ADHD can possibly understand. Do not give me too much in one instruction, you will blow my head up and I will end up in a meltdown. And then I might just slip back into mental self-harming, punishing myself and admonishing myself for not being better at meeting other people's expectations of me, even when those people do not understand anything about me and have totally omitted any consideration for me and my needs or feelings.

How I deal with it?

I make sure everything is broken down into small pieces which are easily achievable and more easily remembered in terms of details for completion.

I reward myself for every task completed, even if it is just an internal 'aren't I great to do that' moment.

I use my mindfulness skills to support my mental attitude of acceptance of self and being ADHD and also to stay focussed.

I keep a diary and try to remember to look at it every morning at least, as well as making a mental list of what needs doing, but I might need lots of prompts to get it done even then. For instance I knew our fridge needed cleaning out and I had ordered a delivery of food, to arrive in three days time, from making that note to myself.

However on the morning something upset my routine and I forgot / procrastinated. But the delivery van turned up too early and drove off again. We saw it from the window. I suddenly remembered I did not want to fill it with new food until I'd cleaned all the shelves etc. properly so I rushed down and frantically started stripping the fridge down. Needless to say I didn't quite manage it in time and David had to come and help me and bring the food in while I pressed on with replacing the now shiny clean shelves back into the fridge. It got done but only with back-up and probably not if the van hadn't turned up early and driven off briefly.

This is the scenario of so very much of my life. It is living with ADHD. Once upon a time I would have been upset and self-harming about it but now we both laugh at it. After all even though David was involved in something of his own at the time, why shouldn't he come and help me out? Instead of viewing it as a failure on my part, it became a willingly fulfilled joint effort we were both equally responsible for. This happens several times a week though.

ND Overload

Too much is happening all the time. You neurotypicals may not recognise this but millions of bits of information are coming at you every second. Your brains can probably filter this automatically and thus you only notice the chosen items. I notice about five times as much as you at least and probably far more than that. This is only the present moment too. For most people you also live in past and future modes, unless you practice mindfulness deeply and are able to stay fully present from choice.

Past present future

We find it harder to consider future issues, consequences and outcomes, and to learn from the past mistakes too – that was then this is now, it's different. Not impossible but harder. Telling us doesn't work either. Being too present without awareness is just as bad as being stuck in the past or dealing with the over-anxiety about the future, and just as disabling. However, as a student of mindfulness, I find it easier to be present most of the time than non ADHD neuro-typicals do. But being consciously present means I am aware there are outcomes I need to consider and lessons to learn that would be helpful to recall. Making them conscious present mind helps me to do that. So I recall the lessons previously learned by bringing them to mind and stating out loud I do not need to repeat this, usually spoken out loud to my husband who is amazingly supportive of the effort I put into being my best self. The other evening I was trying to eat less and avoid gaining older age spread and I knew I was going where sweets are on sale. I said out loud in the car en route that I did not need to do any secret treat eating as I would not be hungry and might enjoy the feeling of losing some of my excess weight. I did not succumb but I know that if I had not stated that out loud as my intended choice of behaviour, my instant gratification delay aversion mind would have said 'no one will know, you can get away with it so just do it.' Consequences are not something we naturally consider, the impulse to do something right away is very powerful. It makes us fun and full of initiative and exciting to be with, but we can also find ourselves in nightmares. We commit whole heartedly to things before we can be certain it is right for us, including relationships/ friendships. It means we get hurt a lot too and our tender hearts are easily damaged in ways that we believe are judgments of us. We begin to feel as if we only deserve to get rejected or hurt or fail because that is what happens to us so very often.

Mindfulness has really helped me in managing these issues and given me a life where I am now free to accept my ADHD and work with it, instead of being filled with shame and self-loathing for it.

The advantage of being present is that you are less goal driven and more easily able to go with the flow in life and deal with things as they actually arrive. This is something many people strive for but with ND, if you can work with it you will achieve it more easily.

I do work very hard to try to strike a good balance between enjoying today and organising for tomorrow. The aforementioned diary is essential. It is hard to disconnect from the distractions and temptations of the moment on my own but here again my wonderful husband is willing to talk it through with me and we create spaces in our relationship, mostly in shared baths where there are fewer distractions for me, where we ponder our options and make joint decisions. Then all I have to do is to remember them.

My diary is my most important tool to survive with. It reminds me of what I must do and when, which order I should do them in. Even the act of writing it down, which is another layer of memory processing, helps me to remember there is something I must remember today. Electronic diaries don't work for me but might for others. I am of my era. My diary is on my table along with last year's one in case I need that one too. That older diary will get put away when I get next year's one ready to start filling in. I am not always on task at checking my diary, but it makes life a lot less impossible for me.

My diary also helps to stop me overcommitting. I easily under-estimate how much time and energy something will take and give myself too much to do. I am very willing and open to helping others but to my own detriment and have had to get a lot better at saying no. I even schedule a nap now most days as I don't usually manage a full nights sleep undisturbed very often and although I can be very productive at night, writing etc, I do need to get enough sleep overall.

Motivating myself

If there is something I want to do then I will probably end up hyper focussing on it anyway. But what if I don't? What if it is less exciting than a hyperfocus potential. I really have to work at motivating myself to get those organised and achieved too. I also programme treats in for myself if possible. I like to take trips away, though this is mostly impossible for us both nowadays especially with environmental issues, but giving myself something great to look forward to always helps me to stay motivated and on task in the present.

Good alternatives for me now are going for walks and a pub meal with good friends. Something that involves movement is essential. My current favourite is my old age ballet classes which I would do daily if available but twice weekly suffices. I never miss them or forget them, and in lots of ways the weekly punctuation mark helps me to stay on track with the rest of the week too. It really is about allowing yourself to focus on what gives you joy and take that as a baseline for other things.

I don't really do 'weekends' as far as getting things done. I work when it feels right and it feels like I could really achieve something.

Finding the right balance

There is a point of balance in everything with ADHD, where the ups and downs meet and we can make the best of it all. This takes careful self-awareness and recognition, understanding of your own unique expression of ND and the demands of your life. Make it simple if you can. Stop punishing yourself for being ND and start to work with it constructively. Work out how to make the best of your ND super-skills and energy and enable those around you to work with you to the best for everyone. Allow others to support you too. It can feel very humiliating to need constant support from others, but it is actually a sign of love and trust and humility, yours and theirs, all of which are really great things to have in life. Those around you and your ND can gain so much if they also learn how to help you make the most of it all and cease the expectations based on their own limited abilities. Yes ND can present lots of problems in life but only if you don't work creatively with it. Once upon a time, humans lived without concepts of time being measured and our ND brains would have been a real advantage then. Let us celebrate them now too. Let us not sweat the small stuff.

7. Living with ADHD – we got married

'Life can only be understood backwards but it must be lived forwards.' - Soren Kierkegaard

Everything I am about to write is true and the names have not been changed to protect the innocent.

For the partner of someone with ADHD the initials stand for Another Day Handling Doubt. Why? Well because the person you love has so often been told not to do the things they do and not to behave in certain ways (that come naturally to them) that consequently they have learnt to doubt themselves and their worth.

How this happens is obvious. At school they are told to stop fidgeting, to concentrate, to behave like their peers. At work they fall into jobs that don't suit their intrinsic nature and become the square peg in the round hole. What chance of success in life when you are constantly being told you are wrong, you have failed, you don't fit in, and yet where would we be without the energy, creativity, and enthusiasm of those who have ADHD?

Often the most creative people, the ones with drive and passion are those who have behaviours attributed to ADHD. We admire those people because they have something we do not, a restlessness that leads to exploration of new ideas, the creative urge brought about by the need to be doing something different all the time, an energy that inspires others. But we only admire them when they have succeeded and this is because we admire what we consider to be success and disparage what we consider to be failure. So what am I suggesting here? I am suggesting that given the right circumstances ADHD can be hugely positive but only if it is recognized and harnessed and nurtured and I am also suggesting that it is never too late, it just takes someone to see things differently. Ok, well there is positive news, now I am going to tell you what it is like living with someone who has ADHD.

You have had a heavy day and sitting on the sofa your partner yawns and tells you she is tired and needs to go to bed. This is a good idea, you feel the same way, you are in harmony. So you get to bed and having had an end of the day cuddle you begin to drift into that hazy realm of oncoming sleep, oh the bliss as you sink down into the silence of endless space. Calm covers your relaxed limbs, thought switches off and there is nothing............

'Do you think your mother would like some honey?'

Your brain crashes into hyperactive mode, believing it is being attacked. The words strike you like a board duster thrown by an angry teacher. Adrenalin floods the nervous system as you scramble to make sense of words that have no meaning. They are out of context, unexpected, demanding a response!

'Honey? Mother?

Having kicked in, the adrenalin wakes you up, fires your thought processes and leaves you in a place of total conflict.

You want to sleep, you were asleep, but now you are awake and for no good reason! Your partner, who had instigated the migration to the bedroom saying they were tired is now fully awake and asking you questions. Now this example is not an isolated incident.

Because like most bedrooms ours is upstairs we eventually dubbed this situation 'altitude sickness'. Downstairs Sylvia was tired, upstairs she woke up, regularly! The questions she asked ranged from the Honey one to things such as 'did you lock the back door', 'do you think the Buddha was right about impermanence', and of course the most annoying one 'are you asleep yet'? The latter one always came on the cusp of sleep immaculately timed to cause maximum effect, and yet there was never any malicious intent. Sylvia didn't deliberately want to wake me, but I could have seen it that way, and in fact did until I understood the nature of her ADHD. In the beginning I used to get so irate I often thought of doing the same to her in return, but of course I always fell asleep before the opportunity arose.

Scattering and untidiness
Let me talk about 'things'. What do I mean by this? Things that have been started and suddenly left as though one has boarded the Marie Celeste. That is, someone has been here and there is stuff everywhere but there is now no one to be seen. Examples of this are, a parcel arrives and the books / plants it contains are unpacked on the nearest surface. The person who has unpacked them has disappeared but the packaging remains. Not only does

it remain, but it continues to remain until……well who knows when? Sylvia is a gardener and a fine one too but as she wanders through the garden if she sees a weed she plucks it out and casts it to the side and it is a good thing to do. However like the packaging, it stays where it has been plucked. We have some stone benches and a small Buddha statue where we can sit and enjoy the garden, for months now the benches have been covered with one of Sylvia's weed collecting forays. They rest like an ill fitting wig that one can't avoid noticing but hesitates to mention. Collections of stones appear on paths where you want to use the wheelbarrow, empty black plastic pots blow like tumbleweed across the lawn. Now I am making it sound like a nightmare but it is not. As I have already said Sylvia is a brilliant intuitive gardener and her sense of colour and design are wonderful and I could just pick up those abandoned weeds, I could sweep the stones, I could put right the very things I am using as examples of Sylvia's distracted nature so why don't I just do that? Why don't I just accept that I see things that she doesn't seem to see? It is an interesting question and one I hope to explore in due course.

What is also truly interesting is that when Sylvia gets the urge to tidy up, the things she sees first are mine! This very morning from a table covered with scattered papers and other objects she brought out a folder of mine and said 'this has been on the table for weeks' and then proceeded into the utility room, the work surfaces of which have been groaning from 'things' of hers forever, and she picked up a paint tray I had left (admittedly some time ago) and said it really shouldn't be there, the room was for working in!

Recap time, people with ADHD are brilliant, they just do things differently and they see things differently.

So if you live with someone with ADHD, one of the things that you will notice is that they start a lot of things and they don't necessarily finish all of them. In the words of the business psychologist Belbin 'they are not completer/ finishers'. This is partly down to distraction e.g. they start something, then get distracted and move on to something else without really noticing it, and it is partly down to boredom i.e. I've done the interesting bits and now this is tedious.

So the positives are they are always busy and the not so positives are it makes you feel like saying 'why don't you just finish what you have started before you move onto something else?'

What a ridiculous thing to say to someone with ADHD!

Those of us who live with someone with ADHD learn to understand that just isn't going to happen. Often any resistance from 'our side' comes from the fact that at times we can feel like we are left to pick up the pieces such as the nettles, the stones and the tumbleweed pots. On the other hand I sit in a beautiful garden, I eat home grown vegetables, and Honey from Sylvia's bees, I eat eggs from the chickens, none of which would have happened without ADHD.

Fair exchange? I think so, but I need to own up to the fact it took me a long time to see it this way, what I initially saw was what was left for me to do when I hadn't actually instigated any of it. They weren't my Chickens, they weren't my Bees, I didn't want three quarters of an acre of garden etc., etc., and yet I was sharing the work involved in these things. It takes a shift in consciousness and a willingness to see that ultimately the drive, energy and enthusiasm will bring you abundance if you only let it.

8. I have ADHD and am highly Sensitive, and it can be really hard to live with it

'That's right' - Authors husband, David.

Is it mainly women or can men be like this too? Though it seems to be mainly female, I know there are many males with ND who are equally sensitive but have learned to conceal it for the sake of their masculinity. I am sure this is true of my sons who have ADHD as they also have many of these symptoms

The modern world is full of loud noises and bright lights. Apparently, this attracts other humans' attention and thus is good for marketing purposes. Witness the sheer volume of advertising in Piccadilly Circus. I can barely cope with walking through quickly on my way to the Royal Academy. Others find it exciting.

Urban life has become utterly chaotic and over-stimulating and this is well documented as being universally harmful to our senses and nervous systems. I used to cope when I lived in South London but I always lived on quiet roads and gravitated towards large gardens and parks. Because I love music, and loud is fine for me with music, it never occurred to me that I was otherwise so noise sensitive. I also love the arts and living in South London gave me such excellent access that I counted myself lucky. I just knew that I was also always drawn strongly to rural and coastal living, especially walking in forests, in the silence that only forests can give you.

My eldest son and his more severe form of ADHD made life as a parent extremely hard and I was barely coping. It got slightly better when I was on my own as a parent with alternate weekends 'off' but only slightly. I still had to cope, though I was not living with being endlessly but unintentionally undermined and unsupported. I also had two hostile mother and mother-in-law relationships to contend with. As throughout my childhood, I was 'on my own'.

Daily living was sometimes a hellish experience. Some evenings I would just sit and cry from exhaustion and overstimulation, burnout, and also have to cope with my inner voices which had adopted my family narrative that I was no good, worthless, and unlovable. I found beta-blockers helped with the anxiety build-ups and resultant insomnia.

Anxious or Hypersensitive

For a long time I just thought I was overanxious and stupid but then I started to change my life, mostly through psychology, philosophy, and the practice of mindfulness. It transformed me and everything around me. It woke me up to my own possibilities and gradually enabled me to become who I am today, far from perfect but at least happy to be me and accepting of myself exactly as I am.

My ADHD diagnosis, in my early/ mid 50's, really helped me enormously. I tried the meds but found they made the anxiety sensitivity worse so that was no good for me. I resorted to relying on my mindfulness practice which I'd developed decades earlier.

And then I read up about Highly Sensitive People and so much made sense for both me and my sons. These are some of the factors I discovered:

clothing. Any scratchy fibres really cause us both discomfort though I have learned a tolerance greater than his. So knitting lovely big woollen jumpers for him never went down well. They were more uncomfortable than my sons could bear but if I wear thick cotton under layers and buy good quality non scratchy wool, I am ok. I find acrylics equally scratchy.

Shoes. I cannot wear high heels, so I just stopped buying them. I feel most comfortable in slippers or boots. In the summer I prefer barefoot so I can make contact with the planet through my feet and I find this very comforting. They prefer only trainers.

Emotional sensitivity. This includes deep sensitivity to criticism, deep empathy toward others' feelings, easily shocked or distressed. Sometimes the focus on coping with your own sensitivity can mean you are not so able to consider others but that does not mean you don't care. Sometimes other people are just too painful. I certainly find this with certain emotional energies which I sense so clearly.

Reacting to situations. Often before thought has a chance to rationalise the contingent circumstances, especially with a quick temper that seems to come from nowhere and confuses or even upsets others, gaining us a label of being self-centred and insensitive, the opposite of what we are really coping with.

Large groups of people. I don't like groups of people even though I tried to pretend I did for decades — I had been brought up with 'what's wrong with you why don't you like xxxxxx' so I did everything I could to cope but nowadays I give myself permission to say no to that sensory over stimulation. It is fine though if it is a poetry evening or listening to David's band, I can immerse myself in the music or words and shut other people mostly out, except perhaps for a companion or two.

Distressing films, media generally. I find myself responding very literally to anything I watch or read and have to be careful to avoid that which gives rise to too much adrenaline or distress. It leaves me over stimulated and unsettled, often with resultant insomnia and internal distress. I get flashbacks from horrific scenes even in fiction; there is little difference between fiction and reality for me

Smells. Especially artificial ones make me gag — I cannot bear perfume that is not very simple and human smelling, and house cleaning products need to be eco-friendly and perfume free or I am very uncomfortable.

Sensory Processing Disorder (SPD)— this is an extreme form of high sensitivity that is most commonly found in autism but it is now being recognised that ADHD can have a similar co-morbidity. It is a neurological condition that means incoming information does not get filtered in the way that others can filter it out and reduce it for their own comfort. I can definitely recognise that in myself to some extent.

If your sensitivity interferes with your normal life beyond an inconvenience, then you most likely have SPD to some degree or another. Make a list of everything that you find difficult to cope with and stop blaming yourself for this. You are not being fussy or difficult, though some may tell you this. Starting to list your triggers can be the start of getting life into a more manageable and self-aware place. I still work with this and gradually I pretty much have it sorted out, regardless of how others consider me.

I do have ADHD, and I have always struggled with hypersensitivities. Over the last sixty nine years, I have found strategies for protecting myself from stress and anxiety. I note my sensitivities and make the needed accommodations. I create boundaries for myself that others may not understand but that is their problem and I no longer allow myself to feel bad about how I am.

I embrace my ADHD and my sensitivity as a gift and seek to work with its benefits, of which there are many, such as intuitive, full of energy, very loving, creative, deeply insightful.

I continue to work to be less reactive and anxious, less ADHD / HSP in public terms.

How to live in a world that creates such distress?
Firstly start to recognise that hypersensitivity often comes with ND. You are not crazy, and you're not being pathetic. Your discomfort and pain are real. Honour that in yourself even if others do not.

Secondly, identify your sense triggers and develop strategies to limit their effects. In other words, plan ahead and don't go to places that will be uncomfortable. Check what you wear, eat, listen to, watch, and who you talk to and spend time with. This is mindful consumption and an area of mindfulness teaching that I gained a great deal of healing from. Make sure the people in your inner circle understand and will not make you feel bad about your sensitivity but will treat it with respect. I also have lifelong PTSD – mostly healed now, but still have to be careful of triggers for that too.

It is possible to work to reduce your sensitivity.
Do not take this as a basis for believing you are abnormal or a problem for others. It is no different than someone wearing

glasses if their eyes are different, or a hearing aid, or using face cream if they have dry skin. We all have our differences and that is what makes being human interesting and great.

If other people give you a hard time, they are being insensitive and unkind, not the other way around. It may not be their fault either, we all need to be a lot more gentle and compassionate with each other and less judgemental.

9. How ADHD views Neuro-Typicals.

'Everyone is the same in the bath.' - David's Mother

I will leave you to work out what that quote actually means whilst I talk about the benefits of being wired differently. We are different, sometimes labelled disabled though in my view this is a complete misunderstanding of what ADHD actually is. It can be a major hassle but not necessarily a disability, but if so, we are disabled in different ways. All through my life I've had to get used to people finding me difficult or being upset by me and telling me why I am wrong, not them.
Well, I have thought about that over the years, and this is my take on being ND.
For starters how do you think it feels to always be in the wrong, every day, regardless of how hard we try to fit in? It is really exhausting, depressing and utterly soul-destroying and those who do not have ND do not adjust their ways to accommodate us. Oh no! They are normal. We must conform to them or accept their judgments.

WELL I AM ABOUT TO CHALLENGE THIS!!!!!
We are all very unique individuals, so each one of us will express our ND differently, just like neuro-typicals are different, if more homogenous as a group.

I am not dis-ablist, but I do get frustrated that society creates disability out of difference. That is not a fair treatment and do you know what — neuro-typicals miss out in so many ways, on us, and by not being more like us.

Honesty.

To me some neurotypicals can be deeply dishonest and difficult to trust. There are of course many exceptions to this experience, but some lie a lot. They call it tact or diplomacy but to me it smacks of dishonesty. Why can't people just say what they mean and what is wrong with honesty, bluntness and openness. Some people really find me uncomfortable because I am so direct. They just don't know how to cope with honesty. They find it intimidating or challenging. Well what does that say about them? I mean if they were more honest themselves then it wouldn't be an issue.

The main reason why those like myself are no good at lying is because we cannot remember all the details that are needed to maintain a lie! And the energy feels all wrong too. It just feels plain awful to lie or pretend anything.

I did learn to lie from my Mother, who lied incessantly to protect her narcissistic personality disorder and to blame me for everything. She lied defensively throughout her life. After all, lying is a defence strategy, albeit not a very good one. So I learnt that lying to protect myself was allowed. Except that with my mother, although she gave herself the right to lie, anyone else lying was a heinous crime, so she told everyone what a terrible liar I was. (I refer you all to the simple rule that what you say about other people is more than likely true of you rather than them.)

I hate lying and one of the reasons I am able to feel to open and relaxed in life is because I refuse to feel defensive any more about being the way I am and I do not lie or pretend to suit other people. Also I do not need to impress anyone anymore either, it is ok to be me. So all the tension and anxiety that builds up around lying is gone. What a relief that was and still is.

I distrust tact too. What are you trying to hide? Don't patronise me and think you need to protect me from your own judgments. They are your judgements and not necessarily true about me. If you are afraid of how I might react, that is your own cowardice, you are not protecting my feelings but your judgemental nature. Politeness. What is that anyway, pretending to be someone you are not, why? Why can't you just be yourself? Your own judgements of yourselves as well as of us cognitive alternatives is the problem. So stop being judgmental and start being open to difference. You will be much personally happier for it too. I promise.

Blurtiness

Being 'blurty' is another aspect of this honesty and impetuosity dimension of ADHD. If I think of something, I will probably blurt it out loud. I don't have much of a filter between brain and mouth, though I do put considerable effort into working on that issue. I often say the wrong thing to people at the wrong time, even if it is true and I am just expressing what is on my mind. This is especially true when I am anxious about something, it just sort of pours out of my mouth. I put myself and sometimes others too, into awkward situations without any intention to do so. I am just saying what is in, or on, my mind.

 I am never intentionally unkind, just blunt and up front and tell it how I see it. I don't do compliments either. To be honest I don't trust them. I always think 'what do you want' when most people pay me a compliment and tend to dismiss them until I know absolutely that they are ruthlessly honest with me. Those compliments and nice things spoken mean the world then, because they really mean something. The same is true of me too. That means people who play socially nice games don't like me but people who prefer honesty recognise the realness in who I am and they will be told, but never unkindly, just honesty. Is this a fault? I don't think so and I have heard neuro-typicals say some incredibly dumb-assed and deeply unkind stuff too.

Energy
Neurotypicals lack a lot of energy compared to us ADHDers. We have more enthusiasm and energy and yet neurotypical attitudes try and stifle that very quality in us through drugs and medications, rather than find ways to creatively channel that energy.
Neurotypicals need to be more open minded and allow us to burn off our energy and then enable us to show them what we are capable of. How do you know what anyone can do if you don't allow them to be natural, and their authentic selves?

To truly choose, to act decisively, to embrace your uniqueness of perspective — this is authentic. Allowing the perceptions of others to determine your behaviour is inauthentic and can remove us from a meaningful life.

This applies to all of us of course, everyone needs to be authentic, and allow others the same rights. We have so much to do and so much to offer. All that potential is wasted by diagnosing us as deficient in some way, when many of us feel it is others who are deficient

Divergent thinking

NDers are brilliant at inventiveness and have more alternative ways of looking at life than some NTers do. Why doesn't the neurotypical world set it up so we can explore and experiment and come up with all sorts of wonderful perspectives for humankind?

Our slightly crazy ways of experiencing life make us great fun, but also very intuitive and alternative. Instead of dismissing us, why not work with us and see how it develops. Some of the best observational humour comes from ADHD. We are different but by drugging us into submission and suppressing our qualities and differences, you lose so much human potential. It is so short sighted but that is how non ND minds and brains work. Forgive us our trespasses as we forgive you!

Judgements

People can be so judgemental, and you will find that we are naturally not, although neurotypical teaching to us is that we should become more like them, so we try to, and that includes judging, mostly ourselves for being different, not fitting in, being made to feel worthless and just plain wrong for being ourselves. What hypocrites! That is not ok for anyone.

We are made to be afraid of being authentic and that is a terrible price to pay for acceptance by others, even if we can begin to achieve it anyway. After all we are fighting our own brains in order to please others, instead of exploring what it can do for us and thus for others too.

Who are people so afraid of anyway? The mysterious other / they?

"They" influence how we perceive ourselves and, therefore, influence how we act. Heidegger

The 'They' refers to everyone and no one. It is some non-existent individual, either public or private, and exists both externally and internally. It is an illusory invention that we all buy into and 'they' do not exist. It is not there when we are born but we are trained to look out for it all through our developmental years so it is as real as anything else we will ever understand.

NDers are taught not to trust their own sense of self and how they feel, yet we can all assess how we feel at a given moment if we learn how to look a little introspectively at ourselves. A stable self-perception, one that isn't easily swayed by "the They" can make a difference.

Anxiety

Anxiety is toxic for ADHDers - that is my experience anyway. And anxiety is what piles up inside us as a result of all the pressure NTers and society in general put us under.

Anxiety makes ADHD differences more pronounced, especially the ones you find most annoying.

We don't need to be anxious. In my own home I am almost without any anxiety nowadays since my husband enjoys my ADHD ness and celebrates my exuberance and differences. So I have no need to feel anxious or worried that what happens next might be yet another source of failure, embarrassment, cause for rejection, judgment etc. I cannot express in words what a revelation and liberation this has been,

If I mess up, sometimes I and sometimes we clear it up. Guess what, he messes up too sometimes, and we might both clear that up also. We are endlessly patient with each other. That is the meaning of the word love in action, love in practical living day to day action. Love is acceptance and embracing all the other person is, including in my case my ADHD qualities. So no anxiety. Imagine how much better we would all feel if it could feel like that for everybody everywhere. It just takes being educated and stop assessing others by your own standards. Both Buddha and Jesus told us not to do this, but humans continue to ignore the best of psychological/ spiritual teachings at their own expense.

One thing I have noticed for myself is that being anxious doesn't stop me, it is like there is a motor going inside me that has decided I will do this thing or take that path and nothing will divert me. More of that from my husband in the next chapter! Sometimes I think it is my muse or spirit guide, or my daimon, but sometimes I think it is just my brain and how it works. As a child I was told off for being wilful, but I don't think I had a choice - it was never calculated or intentional, that I can assure you. Punishment never stopped someone with ASD or ADHD. Strict discipline won't make them change. It is just cruelty against differences.

Procrastination and Shame

The greater burden of shame I carry the more disempowered I am and thus the less able to get on with things that suddenly seem overwhelmingly vast and unsurmountable. So procrastination is not really laziness or avoidance though it may seem that way - but it is a form of self-protection from the devastating effects of shame on our psyche. As I have said before- all humans struggle with shame but having ADHD seems to double that burden. Shame at our projection of a possible failure of outcome, of not meeting other people's expectations and assumptions. Nowadays I mostly don't feel much shame within our home as David no longer does anything to cause that emotion to arise in me, but it does sometimes still come on from outside though that is easier to manage. I still shudder when I remember how much shame was heaped upon me as a child though when I couldn't meet my parents approval. Now it is less procrastination and more about remembering 'to get around to this or that today, please, if I can manage it, and if not- well the world didn't end again did it'. The ubiquitous 'they' can still catch me with shame from time to time though.

Impetuosity

Yes, people with ADHD can be rather impetuous and this can lead them into troubles unforeseen. But is it only NDers who do this - of course not?

As Greta Thunberg says, maybe her autism allows her to see through the bullshit. Chris Packham, Jack Munroe and I all feel the same way. Cut the crap, get out of your ego ways and see what is needed. Stop being socially nice or compliant and start being honest, authentic, unafraid. Do what needs to be done and stop worrying about 'what _**they**_ will think or say'.

My husband's take on living with me is that he will never be bored or slip into decline or lack stimulation or fun or adventure. I will always challenge him and keep him guessing and he can put the brakes on me when necessary, but together we can live a vibrant life into our even older age together, having fun, and never sink into decrepitude.

10. Travelling with ADHD

'If you think traveling is dangerous, try routine, its lethal.' - Paul Coehlo

Before I met Sylvia I had never travelled, so her stories of peeing from a high bridge in the Andes mountains, being watched by a jaguar from the banks of a river, watching giant river Otters and Caiman in an oxbow lake and approaching Matchu Pitchu through the sungate at dawn became the stuff of legend.

Who was this exotic person who had seen and done these things? How come Bognor Regis and Skegness were not enough to fulfil her holiday wishes?

Sylvia got the travel bug when she split up with her first husband and needed a complete break from normality. She booked a trip travelling on the back of a truck in Africa. To me this was a brave thing to do. No companion, no knowledge of the terrain or languages, no washing for days at a time, brave and absolute madness, but for someone with ADHD it wasn't. One of the things ADHD seems to bring is this remarkable spontaneity and with it a lack of reflection on the potential negative consequences of one's actions. If it had been me (and I did split up with my first wife so I can say what happened in similar circumstances) I would have painted the outside of the house, thought of joining the golf club, and maybe booked a weekend in Arundel. Which is exactly what I did, other than joining the golf club, which went nowhere because unlike Sylvia I procrastinate.

Contrast Lions and Elephants at dawn with dried out paintbrushes and a rain damped visit to the Wildfowl Trust. Which of us was right?

Well we both were in our own way but who has the more exciting memories? I will leave you to judge that one.

 Here are some of the places we subsequently went to, New Zealand, Canada, Vietnam, Cambodia, Morocco, Cuba, France, Germany, Belgium, the Netherlands, Sweden, Denmark. What has always been interesting to me is that if someone with ADHD wants to do something, then they have the capacity to do it. In Sylvia's case to plan a holiday, book the tickets and make the arrangements.

For a long time I found it difficult to reconcile this ability with the opposite that seems to be the inability to undertake similar planning when dealing with the day to day aspects of life. Often things are overwhelming.

So you have the contrast of a trip to New Zealand with a trip to the opticians where you can ask time and again 'have you made that appointment' and the answer is 'not yet'.

To the uninitiated it appears to be laziness i.e. I will do something exciting like a holiday but I can't be bothered to do something ordinary, however over the years I have come to the conclusion that it is exactly the level of excitement in a task that determines whether it gets undertaken or not and this is not a conscious thing. People with ADHD don't consciously say to themselves 'oh that's boring I can't be bothered' but something in the thought process does this for them and an extra boost is needed to stimulate the activity necessary to energize them into doing something mundane. They need the dopamine hit to be able to concentrate in the first place.

More procrastination, or not

My observations on this topic don't rest with Sylvia alone. My stepson, who inherited Sylvia's genes, used to be exactly the same. He could plan to travel to Australia, spend a couple of months there, or he could plan to go to a rave for the weekend but ask him to sort out something simple like booking his car in for an MOT, or turning up to an appointment he had made, and he couldn't do it.

Imagine getting your head around this as someone who doesn't have those traits.

The immediate (unspoken) response used to be, 'well you only do the things you want to do!', because how else could it be?

After years of grappling with this conundrum it seems to me that the truth of the matter is something along these lines.

Most people without ADHD manage to do things on an average setting on their wish list, which means they don't really get hyper focused to the point where they just have to do something or they will explode, nor do they do things without considering the consequences. They reflect on things and weight up the pros and cons.

This applies whether it is missing a doctor's appointment where non ADHD persons think 'is it worth the additional hassle of apologizing, rebooking, and perhaps having that sore spot for another week', or whether it is going abroad 'is it worth going into debt for and possibly losing your job because your boss doesn't want you away that long?'.

People with ADHD on the other hand seem unable to switch on the 'what if button?' and even when someone says to them 'what if?' they don't seem able to take it onboard. There is an overriding need to do something and that is that. This is clear from the increased likelihood that they will have addictive personalities. Such addictions ranging from watching TV / computer screens to drugs, alcohol, and high-risk sports etc.

Many years ago Sylvia and I were looking for a house from which to run a retreat center. We looked at a number and amongst them one was the dampest, dirtiest, rottenest place you could imagine and which I thought we had both dismissed. One morning whilst I was still asleep Sylvia sat bolt upright in bed and shouted out 'We've got to buy that house!' Once hyper focused on that house there was no way back. Needless to say we bought it and gave it our best shot but that is another story (another book actually). My point is there seems to be a focusing of the mind on an object or a task to the exclusion of all else. It expands to take up all of the space that might otherwise be filled with questions about the viability of the object/ task or it's risk. All that matters is doing 'that thing' or getting 'that thing', what happens during or after doesn't count for much if anything at all.

 Unfortunately, or fortunately depending on how you look at it this hyper focus only lasts as long as the thing is unobtainable, once it has been achieved there is a need to find something else onto which to latch.

Don't think that one holiday every five years will suffice. This is another reason I don't think laziness accounts for the inability to complete mundane tasks because whatever the nature of your partners ADHD whether it is travelling, gardening, writing, cooking, gaming etc., etc., they will always want the next thing. This isn't greed, it is distraction, it is doing something! People with ADHD can't stand being bored so they either lose themselves in computer games or TV, or else they are looking for something to do and of course traveling, the original subject of this discourse, fits that bill one hundred percent.

I have been a lot of great places I would never have gone to had it not been for Sylvia. I have spent endless hours fighting my own reluctance to go to these places and to spend the money it took to get there, and of course we have had long and interesting conversations about our mutual feelings on the subject.

Would I change anything?

No not really. Only perhaps an earlier understanding on my part of how ADHD can be a really positive thing in anyone's life, and in return an understanding by those with ADHD that their lifestyle can be scary to those like myself who have a brain that reckons up the pro's and con's to everything.

It is this mutual understanding of each other which can lead to a great life and alternatively it is the lack of this understanding which can lead to misery. We need to appreciate each other's position and that can be very difficult when often they are so far apart. The teacher who wants a quiet classroom v's the boy or girl who cannot sit still or focus, the parent who wants their child to be successful like all of their friend's children v's the independent child who just wants to be who they are, the stay at home husband who marries a globe-trotting wife! It can all be done if we just understand the way we each think and what our individual needs are. There is compromise of course, frustration, disappointment, confusion even, but the potential for a real and positive change if we just step back and understand that at any one time we are all doing the best we can both with or without ADHD.

11. Positive Qualities of ADHD

'Fall seven times, stand up eight.' Anon

ADHD is a disability, right? I mean who would want to be labelled with any form of ND? Surely we should feel sorry for people with ADHD. You should feel sorry for me!
 I might punch you if you do though lol. So please don't. I'm not the violent type at all really.
I mean we have this burden to carry and we are — well we are really odd, aren't we? I mean not normal in some way. That is how you perceive us. So it is ok to look down on us/them, and to think of us with some kind of pity whilst seeing yourself as not disabled and thus better than us.
Do you feel lucky not to have ADHD?
I feel sad for your lack but I will not dive into the energy-sapping pool of self-pity and denial, and I prefer if you don't try and push me in either.
Sure, there are a few issues and frustrations that go with having ADHD. One of the biggest for me is that one above, other people and ignorance. The need to use someone else's

difference to underpin your own sorry self-esteem and sense of self-worth.

It has taken me decades to get out from underneath that pile of s*#t and no matter how far I run, there always seems to be a new person to dump a load more on me. Boy do my roses smell good though.

I can find it hard to remember things sometimes, and probably a bit more often than you do. And yes I can get distracted rather a lot; so you are in the middle of saying something and I suddenly change the topic without any notice because a new and more interesting thought just came into my head. That can be annoying for you.

But

Often I am quite funny with it too. Don't take offence, just run with it. Who knows where it may take you and me next. I cannot think in linear ways, I am a scattergun of originality and divergent thinking. Tangents are creative and exciting and interesting. You can take care of the linear stuff for me and I can take you on thought adventures. We can both benefit. But just don't sit there with passive aggressive judgements if I do interrupt you. It just makes me want to NOT SPEND TIME WITH YOU. It won't change who I am or how I behave.

Sometimes I do experience excruciating social anxiety, where I just do not feel safe with other people, but is that surprising when I have been bullied and put down for my ADHD — laughed at and rejected even for it, for my whole life. The biggest culprits of that were my own parents and teachers, those people who are supposed to lead you positively through life. No not for people with ADHD.

Far too often school just becomes yet another place of persecution. For me, though family was the worst — full of endless criticism and rejection and then increasingly violent punishment for being myself, as if beating me would change my ADHD brain wiring style. They truly missed out on an amazing woman, daughter, sister, etc. If you are the parent of someone with ADHD then please learn how to manage and enhance them, not try to make them like you, unless you have ADHD too, then embrace it and work positively with it together. I did not learn this in time for my two ADHD sons but we have repaired the damage and made up for it since then. I was carrying too much baggage from my own abusive childhood, so we had to take the healing journey together. We taught each other and pointed out each other's needs for change and growth. It worked.

Far too many friends have also used me over the years as their pet clown and their own ego-boosting adjunct, i.e. a useful add on to their lives but not part of it. Though I have to take some responsibility for allowing that, as I thought it was all I was worth, that never happens anymore since I found mindful self-acceptance. We are not here to make other people feel better than us. We might be here to liberate them though and to teach them new ways of looking at life and living it themselves. While a person can learn the skills to compensate for its downside, no one can learn the gifts that so often accompany ADHD: creativity, warmth, sharp and deep intuitive skills, high energy, originality, and a 'special something' that defies description.

I am married — second time around, to someone who is the most supportive and encouraging friend/soulmate you could hope to find. I used to ask him why he loved me because I kept expecting him to go, 'do you know what, it isn't you, it's me, but I just can't do this anymore'. That was all I was taught to believe of myself and my value. The same is true of many with ADHD. After 27 years and endless re-assurances that he cannot envisage his life without me in it, and that he actively enjoys me being who I am with all the ADHD and what that brings with it,

I can almost bring myself to trust that now. Some of those former friends are not as lucky and are not in a long-term relationship that is as stable and committed as ours, I am sad for them though now lol.

My husband says I am huge fun to be with and that he will never be bored with me. I am never bored with me around either, unless I am severely constrained. Then I just go for a long energetic walk. But as an adult, I can make decisions to do what I need to do to feed that ADHD spirit of adventure and perpetual growth and development. I am not particularly ambitious, but I am very enthusiastic — I just like doing and making things all the time.

I still get really excited like a child does. I am 6 at the point of writing this. It has never worn off. Once, when my son and grandson were due to arrive, I had to run around the house in laps a few times to burn off some of the enthusiasm energy building up inside me so I didn't swamp them when they got here. As I have already said, sometimes I have to stand behind my husband with my hands on his shoulders and jump up and down on the spot just because I feel so enthusiastic about how much I love him.

I can so hyper-focus when it matters and when something gets to me. I can get so absorbed in a film or book, that becomes my reality and I start talking as if that is real. My husband has to say to me, 'that is a story and this is life'. I get so absorbed in films at the cinema that I jump out of my seat and shout out loud when shocked, as if it is real.

When I am on a writing or gardening project, my hyperfocus means that nothing else matters until that target is completed. Unfortunately, nowadays my back doesn't quite agree and stops me early on gardening stuff. Very annoying, as I am left champing at the bit for possibly up to two more days before I can go at it again. But writing takes up my slack and my head is always soooooo full of swirling ideas that I stack them up in the drafts section in notebooks. The backs of novels and other books I am currently reading are full of poetic jottings. I will never run out of ideas, just time and physical constraints to get them all done as my body stops me going at things too hard all the time. I also love silence, on my own or between friends. I love to be able to be silent and in companionship with my close friends whom I do truly love. I don't need to make an external noise all the time, my head is loud enough for me already.

I am fiercely loyal, kind and helpful. I love to help people. Not out of any do-gooding motivation but just because I like to do things that are positive and helpful. I don't mind who for. I love people even if I am afraid of some of them some of the time. People have also done me a great deal of harm, some of it based on my having ADHD and them thinking that I have no feelings to consider or that matter since I am such a clown, in their eyes. They are so deeply wrong. I am highly sensitive and deeply intuitive, though I denied that part of myself for many years in my attempts to conform.

I believe that many people with ND are also like this — very open and highly sensitive people who are not able to demonstrate it in accepted ways and are thus written off. We learn to become resilient over time, to survive, but how many of us also have PTSD as a result of that continuous stream of unskilful words or actions.

I have to be careful about how I expend my energy since in the past I got hurt very, very, very, badly. I do not for one minute think I'm alone in this. I tell my story to speak out for all those others who are not yet able to. ADHD is great but the only real problem is other people who are ignorant, not those who are able to run with us but those who would make us run at their pace. I ask you what are you afraid of, keeping us under control?

We are great in a crisis.

I have really shown how much I can be there for friends when they need me, and then find myself not knowing how to cope when it is all resolved. When normal brains get into overload, we are just hitting our stride and can take it comfortably under our wing and manage to juggle all the needs at once. It is almost what we are designed for, extraordinary needs to focus and juggle massive amounts of inputs very quickly and reliably. When others are in crisis we can be cool, calm and under control, and we rarely miss a thing ever. There are a lot of ADHDers amongst front line service jobs such as emergency doctors and nurses, police officers, fire and rescue personnel, journalists, stock traders, professional athletes, and entertainers. Then there are the creatives like me, possibly. Perhaps these jobs should be reserved for people with ADHD. Just a thought.

Creativity

Have I said how creative we NDers can be, able to think outside the box and follow divergent trains of thought in preference to linear thought processes. I think so! However creativity is expressed, and whatever skills are developed, it always starts with an idea and the interesting execution and development of those ideas.

I love my ADHD and all the gifts it has brought to me.

I love being loved by someone who also loves my ADHD, but I am under no illusions of how hard it was to get here and how many people threw obstacles in my path, hoping I would fall over them, who egged me on, then could or would not celebrate my successes, my achievements. That did not fit in with their story about me, their version of me as a clown and someone who met their need to be entertained by me but not to intrinsically value me.

If you want to really get to know someone with ADHD, and experience how amazing they can really be:

- take time to understand their unique way of being in the world and do not judge them by your own standards
- listen to them and what is in their hearts
- allow them space to be themselves in their fullness not just edited versions to meet social expectations

- don't treat them like exhibits or clowns, or casual entertainment- we might laugh to hide our shame, but you are hurting us and badly.
- respect them for their struggles to survive in a hostile social world and support them in their endeavours
- be grateful to them that they are opening up to you, their natural openness is one of the gifts of ADHD that we have to close down so often in self-defence.

If you cannot do this then at least leave us alone to be ourselves, but you might be missing out on the best friend you could ever have.

I cannot speak for all people with ND. We are all individuals, just like neuro-typicals after all, but we do have much in common and many of those are bad experiences. It isn't necessary, but it's up to you too. We can all be part of the change to an all-embracing, allowing kind of human collective. I believe that bringing out the best in neurodivergent people will bring about a surprising change for the best in all society.

12. Confession Time

'It is better to offer no excuse than a bad one.'

George Washington

Editing this book has made me realise that I have at times been the person who has done all of the things that Sylvia has written so passionately against. George Washington's quote can be read a number of ways but I think what it says to me is don't bother offering excuses, be honest, and so I will. In the distant past, when Sylvia and I first met, I had never heard of ADHD.

Should I have? It wasn't a generally accepted term back then and so when it did come into our lives it came with reservations on my part. What did it mean? Was it another of these Americanisms, some sort of invention of the pharmaceutical industry created in order to peddle Ritalin (also unknown to me at the time).

Or was it another convenient label on which to hang any number of excuses as to why someone misbehaved, lacked self control, couldn't stand being bored, underperformed etc., etc. After all if someone annoyed you when they weren't diagnosed would they stop annoying you when they were? Surely my relationship to my wife or stepson's behaviour didn't depend on initials after their name as if they had suddenly been given a clinical OBE. Why should I suddenly have to put up with untidiness, missed appointments, erratic behaviour, bad money management, a lack of interest in things that didn't seem new and shiny? This was a con wasn't it? Why couldn't I have some initials after my name that meant I could be disinterested in fixing the house, going to work every day, cleaning up the kitchen every evening and breakfast time?

I don't remember expressing myself in this way but I do remember feeling a sense of frustration, anger, self pity (?)…….shall I go on? I think that is probably enough, you get the gist. The problem is that giving someone a label may be useful for the dispensing of drugs but it doesn't mean that the effects of their behaviour are negated just like that. Anyone with a diagnosis relating to behaviour has to be aware that their behaviour impacts on other people. Sylvia has talked about the impact of people on her and I totally understand the effect that has had on her but conversely those with ADHD or similar diagnoses have an equal and opposite effect on the people they live with.

Sylvia's parent's / family did not know she had ADHD (in those days it was not a recognised condition), but they did know she didn't behave 'normally' and her impact on them in part led them to behave the way they did. Look at any child with ADHD who is in or has been through the education system and you will find a child that has probably been labelled disruptive. School is not designed for different children. Teachers cannot afford disruptive elements in the classroom. They're not given the training or resources, and haven't the time or energy to deal with it and for this reason the individual often feels they were punished unfairly whilst the school feels the child negatively affected the education of the other children. Touché.

What I am getting at is that any understanding of ADHD has to be two way. The person affected by the behaviour of an ADHD diagnosed person has to understand why they behave that way, and on the other hand the person with the ADHD has to understand how their behaviour affects others, and then they have to work together. It is only through mutual understanding and joint effort that anything positive can come about. The ADHD label cannot be an excuse for continuing 'difficult' behaviour without any responsibility on the part of the ADHD individual, just as endless condemnation without understanding cannot be the position of those who deem themselves to be 'normal'.

How did I get over the problem I had with ADHD as a cop out? It took a long time and especially so as my stepson (with whom I have a very good relationship nowadays) caused me endless worry. His mother, as most parents would, defended him when I got cross and of course at the time what I did not realise was that they both had similar behavioural traits. Somewhere deep down Sylvia understood where her son was coming from. Here is a list of some the problems we faced.

- Inappropriate use of drugs and alcohol

- The inability to hold down a job

- Impulsivity i.e. just taking off somewhere at a moments notice

- Spending money that didn't exist

- Repeating things that he had been asked not to do

- Crashing cars

- Not finishing jobs he had been asked to do

- Inviting persons unknown to us to stay at the house

I won't go on but anyone who knows about the behaviour of those diagnosed with ADHD might recognise similar traits in people they know. For me it was just belligerent behaviour, a self-centred 'I don't care what you want or think' attitude, and as a non-paying guest in our house! I should add here that my stepson was in his late twenties when he came to live with us following some bad things happening in his life elsewhere. My memory is not good enough to pinpoint where and when I finally understood what was happening, but part of that learning curve involved joining Sylvia in teaching Mindfulness to groups with ADHD as part of research she was involved in with Southampton University. We had been teaching Mindfulness for years (before it became the buzz word) and it had been fairly straightforward but when we began to teach two groups, one adult based in Bristol and one children on the Isle of Wight everything became really quite different. For one thing Mindfulness is based on focussing the mind, bringing it back to the present moment, for another there are the periods of sitting meditation. Not exactly ideal for the person with ADHD. But the thing which really struck me was when they talked about their experiences of the exercises and life generally, as one does when undertaking mindfulness training, I could see my stepson and Sylvia so clearly in these two groups of people. Their lives overlapped so much that there had to be common ground and that was of course their ADHD behaviour.

I was at last beginning to see that I wasn't being duped or taken for a sucker. The way Sylvia and my stepson lived their lives it seemed was not uncommon, as the two groups showed. In the adult group were artists and scholars as well as those with 'ordinary' jobs and those who couldn't manage to hold a job down, a wide spectrum of people coping with life with ADHD but having a common experience of the difficulties it presented. Distraction, forgetfulness, restlessness, running alongside creativeness and a zest for life but with the desire to have some control over their frustrating traits and that was why they were trying Mindfulness. If you want me to tell you how it all ended for everyone, I can't. For various reasons Sylvia had a breakdown that developed from her PTSD and had to give up her research, one of the great regrets of her life, but if nothing else it enabled me to rethink my ideas about ADHD and to start to ask the question 'how do I begin to relate differently to what was happening'. Instead of moaning about what I saw as problems how could we all work together. I said nothing directly but began to change my approach. They were both going to forget appointments, they were both going to hyperfocus on things they were interested in and neglect the mundane, they would both be impulsive and perhaps spend more than they should. I needed to accept this and, if I could, in a gentle way, point out what their actions were doing to me as the situations arose. I was not as skilful as I wish I could have been and the whole process was a bumpier road than I would have liked, but at least it was going somewhere and that was a start.

13. The Unintentional and Casual Cruelty of Normalcy

'You do not move forward by following convention. You celebrate those who are different, who are not burdened by normality.'   Morten Tyldum

Are you normal? How do you know?

I am not normal but I look as if I should be, privileged even, a good bone structure, well dressed with an innate sense of style, even when scruffy, and when you hear my voice, a well spoken articulate middle class accent. 'She must have it all'.

Well I do and I don't. I have now got to a place in my life where I do have it all, on my terms, but the journey to get here was an endurance and I am glad it is over, the worst of it anyway. But it has left its mark too of course. I am not unscathed. I am a great deal wiser though, and that is a fair exchange.

So I am not normal by the standards usually applied to that concept.

And so probably are you — not normal I mean. You — like me-probably look as if you should be but may well not be.

A friend recently suggested that I mention my ADHD and PTSD rather often. It was an observation and not a criticism. I replied that I knew this and did it because it is a huge part of who I am. I try to inform others for many reasons

1. They may not judge me so harshly. As is often the case when I act 'out of character', it is their expectations of me that I am contradicting. That would be what they think 'out of character' should be though, because for me it will be in character — probably. Either that or an anxiety response to their expectations of me, or anxiety generally anyway.
2. If I am a little odd, they do not think it is their fault or they have done something wrong. I am just a little weird at times and it is not them. I don't want other people to feel uncomfortable because of me!
3. It enables a conversation about diverse life experiences.
4. It opens up the whole debate around differences and their perception in society. It makes it an open topic instead of a 'behind hands, gossip and patronising sympathy' one.
5. I still feel the need to justify and explain myself to everyone as I still find it hard to accept my own 'acceptability' to others. Sometimes you cannot please everyone and some people are just jerks anyway —

although I prefer to think of them as misguided or uninformed individuals.

In some ways that latter point is the point I want to pick up on in this chapter. So many people, and sometimes on a 'multiple times a day' basis, have made me feel wrong- just plain wrong to be me, to be alive, to be as I am.
I am talking about nice kind straightforward people who just do not understand or cannot stay open to the kinds of differences that people like me might throw up. And I have also heard these same people express concern at how challenging these people, i.e. ones like me, can be and how they need preparation to cope with us. They need warning! Not us who needs to be warned, 'look out guys - you're about to be emotionally abused yet again'.
Their sense of normalcy imposes a burden on people like me to always feel in the wrong, to always feel like we have to justify ourselves or accept what are often patronising attitudes. I have walked away from so many organisations and groups just to get away from that lack of open awareness, what I call the curse of normalcy. It is like living the nights of a thousand knives on a

daily basis. The difficulty they have with us is nothing compared to the difficulty we have with non-ADHD, ASD, PTSD people etc, all the so called normals.

I met a lovely young teenage woman with Downs syndrome. But I could see already she assumed she had to be treated differently and this was not doing her any favours in terms of her socialisation with peer groups. In fact it was disabling her, not her condition but her expectation of being treated differently, specially, over protectedly and not allowing her to learn from life as the rest of us have to.

Of course Downs is more visible but it is still something that happens once people know you have ADHD. It is like a switch goes on in them that says 'not normal'. You can see it in their faces sometimes, accompanied by a slight shadow of fear. Or a sense of judgement. You would be surprised how many people are still prepared to say to me that ADHD does not really exist - try living with it!

I don't want people to know I have ADHD and residuals of PTSD but I feel compelled to tell in some situations and yet equally compelled to pretend I am the same as others, being always caught between the rock and hard place in this set-up. Easiest just to walk away.

There are some who simply like me a lot anyway, we just click and they treat me as who I am — my quirks are part of my charm, part of why they like or love me. There is no patronage or special way of talking to me — and because I am so relaxed with them I am so much less likely to do anything outlandish anyway as anxiety increases the expression of both PTSD and ADHD a hundredfold.

To me the problem is not that we are different, or that others cannot be open and accommodating enough, it is with the notion of normal.

If people don't have this toxic expectancy of some kind of normal, they don't expect anything specific and are thus more open to the amazing diversity of all humanity, equally. If we stop limiting what people find acceptable in behaviour terms, (without of course embracing the 'no nos' like overt and callous cruelty and abusive treatment of others, blatant dishonesty - mostly how politicians behave), we can live with a system that allows a full range of norms across a spectrum that leaves no one out.

We need to keep challenging this notion of normal until it is broken down into something people want to avoid as a label, rather than seek. 'Oh my God you are so normal — how terrible for you.'

As I write this I can feel the anxiety rising in me about a decision I have to make. I stood up and spoke out about a discriminatory rejection made against me, based on judgements of people who barely knew me. Those who had put me forward thought it was absolutely right and were as shocked as I was at this rejection, or rather 'until I had mastered this set of skills'. But the perceived problem was a toxic mixture of my anxiety about being assessed which makes my ND symptoms magnify a great deal in certain situations. It remains unlikely that I am ever going to be able to put on the performance they all expect from me so that I can conform to their sense of expected normal. I could drug myself through it of course.

I challenged them under the Disability Equality Act which states that no one can be rejected on the basis of their disability. I had been open with those who knew me, but the whole organisation was not in the know and I didn't want them to be. But now they all are — which I decided to do to try and make sure no one else ever went through the intense pain and suffering and sense of worthlessness that this 'event' reduced me to. I am not allowed to know the identity of those who made that rejecting decision, so I am left still not trusting mostly everyone. I was persuaded to continue with my membership request and that it is all now agreed, and yet language comes out of that same organisation which shows they have not learned anything — or certain amongst them have not anyway. But the anonymity makes it impossible for me to prepare myself or to cope with the pressure without my nervous system erupting all over the place and I just don't want to go through that.

I am still sad that none of them have had the courage to talk to me in person about their original decision or make any sign that they have any understanding or regret or learning from that. I also distrust that lack of transparency. It is all so patronising and controlling.

Shall I again just walk away from yet another thing that would have meant the world to me, or dig deeper than any of them have ever had to, to find the courage and strength to face them down and go ahead anyway. I know I also have supporters so I am not isolated, and in fact have been led to believe I am wanted by those I know. There are other ways of achieving my goals anyway.

I write this up in more detail to demonstrate the kind of dilemmas we face daily. Belonging is so often denied out of ignorance, but those in ignorance do not want to admit as such. But it is an example of what non normal ND people go through every day and I want to open up this conversation more and more widely, to encompass all sorts of differences and embrace this wonderful genetic diversity that is in fact normal as a genetic expression of the human race and its evolutionary potentials.

14. Repeat after me

'To know all is to forgive all.'
Anon

In the last chapter Sylvia talks about her difficulty with judgement and with fitting into the 'normal' world especially with groups and organisations, and this has been a feature of our relationship on and off since its beginnings.

For this reason I think it is probably a good idea to talk a little about an outsiders perception of the problem. As with all of the topics we are covering in the book I have to make it clear that these are just my observations and are not based on anything other than personal experience.

There may be many people with ADHD who have no problem with groups etc., and are able to 'fit in' easily, I hope so.

Here are some of the groups Sylvia has been involved with over the years :-

- Writing groups
- Family support groups
- Women's hostels
- Garden societies
- Buddhist and other spiritual development groups
- Arts foundations
- Hospital chaplaincy

There are others but these are just a few of the varied voluntary groups I am aware of. Of course they only represent her outside interests. Sylvia was a college teacher for many years and so had to fit in with the structures of the educational system with all of its restrictions. What can possibly go wrong with putting a person with ADHD into a situation where there are rules, deadlines, hierarchical structures, egos, expectations? Have you ever seen a caged Tiger pacing up and down, or a Killer Whale in an oceanarium? Both can be taught to perform tricks but neither is very happy, and one day......... I think you get the picture.

Over the years I have become used to Sylvia announcing that she is going to do this or that thing, to embark on some new venture. This is natural for someone with ADHD. They like new things, they like a challenge, they have enthusiasm for the next thing in their lives. These admirable qualities are only matched by their overwhelming propensity to choose ideas that are incompatible with their basic nature because they often involve organisations.

Definition :- Organisation
A structured group of people working towards a mutually accepted goal with defined rules
Synonym :- Planning, co-ordination, logistics, establishment, regulation

Anyone spot the issue here? In case you haven't I will give you a clue, 'rules', 'planning', 'logistics'. Now I have never actually read the DSM-5 cover to cover (the diagnostic manual for psychiatric disorders) but I don't think under ADHD it says 'remarkably good at obeying rules, planning ahead, and obeying regulations.'

Don't get me wrong, I am not suggesting that people with ADHD aren't good for organisations, I am suggesting organisations aren't good for people with ADHD, and here is the crux of the issue. Don't get people with ADHD to organise your events if they don't have sufficient admin backup. Don't ask them for their opinion if you don't like hearing something different, don't ask them to be treasurer if you don't like constructive accounting, but do use their enthusiasm, do listen if you want to hear something out of the box, do employ them if you want someone who can hyperfocus and will put heaps of energy into a project.

Sylvia and I have discussed this issue a lot over the years, specifically when things go wrong. I don't know whether we have reached a mutual understanding or not, but I think we are getting there. My stance used to be 'why do you keep joining groups?' Her stance was 'why shouldn't they learn to understand me?' Both valid viewpoints but I guess in the end neither solve the problem. At the end of the day my take on it is why put heaps of energy trying get yourself slotted into that round hole when it's not going to be comfortable sitting in it anyway? It's like the old debate of equality for women. Do you like where men are that much that you want to be equal to them or isn't it better to be different but to insist on having the same life opportunities? It is a question of acceptance as much as equality i.e. I am different to you, I am a woman accept me for my incredible qualities. I am different to you, I have ADHD accept me for my incredible qualities. Don't try to get the system to fit you in, fit into the system where you are at your best then change the system elsewhere.

15. So you want to be friends? (making relationships with someone wired differently).

> *"Sanity is madness put to good uses."* George Santayana

You feel attracted to me. You think you might want to be friends, or more? Wonderful, but before you get carried away, let me give you a word of advice. You appear to be mostly normal. Our interests are potential areas of compatibility. I can come across as normal too – to begin with, but there is far more to the story. So this is who I am. Are you also hiding a similar secret, or are you really the same as everyone else, neurotypical and untraumatized?

    Really!!!!

We have some things in common, like perhaps beekeeping, gardening, writing, music, dancing, spiritual / psychological interests. You seem like someone who could develop into a confidante and who could share horror stories and laugh with me over mine. We could support each other in those loving and accepting ways.

__But I come with a health warning, I have ADHD and easily re-triggered PTSD, though that second issue is getting easier.__

Before we make tentative forays into tentative friendship, there are some things you need to know, so that it doesn't ruin the thing we've got going on, about what friendship with me will possibly involve. Are you up for it, because if not then turn away? I shall be fine if you do. I am used to this reaction at all stages of friendship and relationships. It has happened to me more times than I can remember. I accept that I am like marmite and that is fine with me.

You see there will be a lot of advantages to you as well as some challenges. It is up to you to decide if you are up for it or not.

Making arrangements

1. I will be late or not, or early, or forget completely.

I'm continually worried that I will be late so I am usually slightly early but if I am too early I worry that I might get distracted and forget, so I just leave and then I won't be too late. Being late is disrespectful. I know this. It is saying to someone 'your time doesn't matter'. This is not how I feel about you or anyone and not myself either. So please don't be late for me either. It drives me nuts, though I do cope with it.

But if I am not early I might have forgotten completely. I make plans and put them in the diary, but if I have too much to remember then I forget things and other distractions and priorities take over.

For instance, one day a while back now, I had made plans to see someone for lunch but I had the back of my car full of stuff for a charity shop, which I had to remember to drop off on behalf of someone else. I had finished my shift at the hospital where I worked as a chaplain, and often feel rather preoccupied after that, so I forgot about the meeting until I saw a message on messenger, and then I was horrified at what I had done and wanted to make amends. And that very long sentence is what it is like inside my head all the time, and worse.

2. I can be forgetful, or over remember details.

   I have a brain that over remembers details like a fixation or a hyperfocus on somethings and then I completely forget other things. My brain focuses on what it wants, not what I want. It does its own thing and can be very frustrating so I might not remember anything you said about this or that, or I might remember down to how you sneezed when you were telling me, but I won't know which until you try and continue that conversation at a later date.

   When making social arrangements I try really hard to be prepared, to pack bags, to collect everything expected of me. My house is often piled up by the front door with things I must remember to take, and then I walk right past them and forget them on the day. I might have to run home. You might be kind enough to lend me something for the tenth time. For that, I will be eternally grateful. I do get there in the end, but it can take a few goes at it.

3. I will interrupt you with a completely unrelated thought – often

You will be talking about something important in your life. I'll nod and hhmmm, and agree, and when you pause, I will start to talk about something that happened to me last week, perhaps similar to what you were talking about because you triggered that thought in some way, and that thought is right now dominating my brain. It is not that I don't care about what you are saying. I work very hard at refraining from this, but it happens.

This is incredibly rude. I should still be concentrating on you and I have trained myself to concentrate on what people tell me, and I really do care, but that thought came on so suddenly, and so strongly, that the need to tell you super-ceded all social convention. I'm not ignoring you. I am not obsessively self centred. My conversational skills just misfire – sometimes badly. I work very hard at not doing this but sometimes it just happens anyway.

4. I am a very good friend

Once you get to know me, I am a very good friend. I am fun once I know I can trust you. I don't always meet new people easily because I am afraid they might trigger my PTSD, which is very uncomfortable. I might seem wary and quiet to you. I can chat with you until the sun goes down. I am loyal, I am funny, but I have got ADHD and had a breakdown from PTSD, which still sometimes gets triggered. It makes me who I am, but it can also make me seem uncaring, self-centred, or downright frustrating. It also makes me endlessly compassionate and understanding about other people's struggles and issues. Make sure that you know that before going into this friendship. We can be great friends but remember ADHD and PTSD will always be part of the equation. Once I know I can feel safe with you though, once I know you will value and understand me and won't get too angry with me for being weird sometimes, you have someone who will always be utterly there for you and will love you deeply as a friend.

5. I get weird sometimes

Mostly due to my PTSD history, but sometimes I am feeling really vulnerable and insecure, and will come over as slightly monosyllabic. Once I know you it will probably not be with you, but because we are with someone else with whom I do not feel safe. I am not good in crowds and they leave me feeling overwhelmed and my usual extrovert fun loving personality disappears and instead I may appear sullen and quiet and detached. This is just my way of coping with things that make too many demands on me. Alcohol does this to me too. In the past some unkind people tried to get me drunk to make me even more zany, and all it did was to make me quiet instead. They were always disappointed.

If you are my friend, you must somehow know that none of this is about you at all, just me and my way of coping. Also my very best favourite times of all are one to one with my husband or a close friend, or two other friends as a pair of couples. I like to meet people through doing things and then move on. I used to make connections with people but don't do so as much nowadays, since that breakdown. It is over and I am quite well now though.

6. Oversharing

I am not very good with boundaries and when I am especially pre-occupied or anxious about something, I tend to hyper-focus on it and will sometimes blurt out stuff to the wrong people. I work very hard not to do this and it is another reason I don't like groups or crowds of people. Blurtiness at inappropriate times/ things/ people is a real problem for most people with ND. However if you share something with me in confidence I am able to hold that for eternity as it is not about me.

16. The joys of ADHD (with intentionally unedited typos)

'It is not our differences that divide us, it is our inability to recognise, accept and celebrate those differences.'

Andre Lourde

Imagine living in a world where almost everybody speaks a slightly different language to you and no matter how hard you work at it you cannot make out what they are talking about. Of course it is not a language of words but a language of social rules and expectations, of behaviours, assumptions and understanding which just are invisible to my brain. My brain is utterly literal, ruthlessly honest and outspoken, and impulsive, act / speak now and sort out the mess later if I need to, or die with shame of course.

Please can someone give me a dictionary of social cues that I can carry with me at all times and when faced with people who don't know me, I can use to decipher what they really mean, and then give me tips on how to respond.

Please can I also have an emergency button when things are happening too subtly or quickly for me to notice, so I can freeze it while I work out how to manage this so that people don't get annoyed with me or misinterpret my intentions from their own approach to life.

Your normal brain might be busy, but my brain is competing in fast sprint races non-stop. It never ceases.

Even when I sleep, my dreams are often frenetic. But not just my dreams. I can hear my thoughts racing while I am asleep more often than not , and if I am woken up by something, there they are, racing away with such a rush to get out into the world of consciousness, all jostling for space and attention. They literally never stop.

This is why I like being alone, being quiet, being away from people. I like people in ones and twos, two couples even. That can be great because the social cues are not coming too thick and fast for me to cope, and if they know me they may already be predisposed towards my openness and upfront nature of being. My husband certainly says that is one of the first things that attracted him to me.

I can't do subtle very well either although I have been working on that for the last 6 decades too, but I am now in my 7th and have decide to just accept this is how I am and I shall stop trying to be a conforming 'different me' in order to fit in with others. I shall graciously allow them to fit in with me instead, or not. If they don't want to, that is fine too. I actually do have enough friends and loved ones to feel blessed, so more is not necessary. Self-acceptance is key to living well with ADHD and being yourself in all your glory. It is a key principle in mindfulness teaching too.

My meditation practice is of stopping and re-focussing, again and again and again. Like most people, my mind still wants to run off and do its own thing. Actually it wants to do 50 million other things, but I have learned to bring it back again and again and again to this breath, this single moment of experience. Believe me it works. That is how I collect my thoughts enough to write them down, although they do tumble out at an incredible rate once I have my theme and the typos are astonishing. I am actually extremely good at spelling but my thoughts come too quickly to be able to get my fingers around the keyboard to keep up with them and I have to go back and unpick what some words are actually meant to be. I jokingly call my typing dyslexic finger syndrome- DFS.

I have tried to type more slowly on the basis that it takes me longer to go back and make all the corrections which I don't always see either. My brain is very good at gestalt, at seeing what I think is there rather than what is actually there. I am brilliant at reading those pieces of writing where half the letters are missing or incorrect and not noticing it because my brain goes straight to the intentional content. Capitals in the middle of a sentence are just annoying and are not necessary. There should be no I — it should be i instead, then humans, or english speaking one's at least, might not have such a problem with the ego and a sense of superiority. Just be a little old i, and then my typos need fewer corrections too. I shall leave them for the rest of this piece and see how you manage with that. I could leave all the typos uncorrected and see how you manage to interpret my meanings lol.

Many people write about how ridiculous it is to try and teach meditation to people with ADHD because we are the last people on earth who will be able to achieve it.

I disagree, profoundly.

Having ADHD does not make it impossible to concentrate or train the mind, just a lot harder. But we are also experts at it. We are managing it all the time, as a constant barrage of management demands — and it is exhausting. When there is too much going on outside though, my brain just closes down in protest.

Parties argghhh!!!!!

Why?

Why do you want to fill a room full of people all making noise, and then add music to that, and then expect anyone to hold a proper conversation? And what on earth is the point if you don't want to have a proper conversation? There are too many other actually interesting things happening to be bothered by such things. I am probably more interested in the contents of my nose and why they are almost black when i am in London and pretty pale when i am at home. THe my mind goes onto polution adn the state of the world and famine and organice farmign which woudl be so much better and wiser o adopt globally but big business and macho banking ad usiness attitudes need bigger nadcheaper andmroe profit to eb what drived everything, how shallow is that.

Did you like my typos there????

Oh i see you are still wanting to tell me something about your house/ child/ grandchild. OK i shall conform and work very hard to listen- which is exhausting but worth it because then you might be interested in listening about mine. But are you really — i don't think so. Only if you are already a true friend of mine with an investment of time spent listening and learning about our mutual lives and listening deeply to our concerns as well as our joys. We all have our stories but why don't you want to listen to them properly and only wear your social body armour. That is something i don't have you see. I am open and raw and present all the time. I cannot cope with the usual social rounds because they assault my senses and sensibility and then i get told i am insensitive or too sensitive or both at the same time even which doesn't make sense but that is what i am told, by people who think i need to understand that and then can suddenly somehow stop being like that. Sorry mate — no can do.

What you see is what you get — pretty much that is it. Over years i have learned a little discretion and circumspection but only if I am very relaxed. Add any kind of anxiety or stress to the mix and that goes out of the window. But in my world those social skills are irrelevant anyway, why would you want that when they are open to abuse by dishonesty and pretence and social superficiality, why would anybody want that for a minute. Oh yes i forgot it is part of your body armour and people like me offend you because we see right through it or walk right through it even — metaphorically speaking.

You see that is the part i don't understand. You without ND may be in some sort of majority but not that much — so why are your social rules the 'right' ones and not ours? Why is our openness and straightforwardness the so called disability and not your emotionally constipated, closed down, dishonest ones. Oh some people with ADHD do lie and do it all the time. They have learned that from you though, and they do it to protect themselves from your judgements and hostility and rejections, your treatment of us a class clowns, problems, and social curiosities. We have to protect ourselves from you and that is acceptable but if you have to cope with us then we are a nuisance???

Sometimes also i try and explain all this to someone and they might say oh yes i am like that too and i learned to do this or that or the other. Great. For you i am very pleased. For you. I just ask that you hand me that encyclopaedic dictionary of what to look out for and the magic freeze button so i have time to look it up and remind myself what the rule is here or there too. quickly now i don't have time to wait — i might make another social gaffe in the meantimes and have to endure the censure yet one more time.

Oh the endless censure, it is so debilitating. It triggers so much shame too. It achieves nothing.

Do you know what it feels like to pick yourself up again and again and again and somehow face the world, knowing you will also face the social censure which is part of your daily landscape, until people get to understand you as you are and you can relax with them? Such friends are oases in the world of constant anxiety, treasures beyond belief. They like me for who i am, ADHD and all.

So forgive me if i get defensive sometimes. I don't have the body armour to protect me like you do and your attitudes to me really really really hurt, but i have learned to accept that as normal. I have learned to expect it, even from people who are so called compassionate buddhists or quakers or other groups of well-meaning self-satisfied people who have a tradition that make them think they are better than that. To them we are still the difficulty — not their lack of openness of flexibility which we have struggled to learn, to cope with them.

I don't blame you/ them. Compassion requires experience as well as loss of self and if you don't have a self then you are enlightened in which case i am just as normal as anyone else to you. If you are not enlightened then you will just not find us that easy but you think we should find you easy — after all you are in the majority.

Us cognitively different ones, on various spectrums, or scales of not normal- we are the anomalies — why should coping with you be a problem since you are the normal ones. Yet you are just as alien to us as we are to you and even if you do have some of our issues, that is our shared humanity — but differences of scale are enormous. Would you believe how many eyebrows raised, sighs of disbelief and contempt and frustration we have to endure from you lot? If you met that daily, as we do, you would be defeated very quickly I am sure. we develop the 'begin again' regime of mindfulness as a matter of survival, some with awareness and some with headlong dives to the next to get away from the last disaster, with the 'sighs' - your sighs - ringing in our ears- always. But sometimes we just can't do it any more. Sometimes it is just too much effort and we have to make the assessment if it is worth it.

People with ND and especially ADHD endure, or sometimes we don't. We escape into alcohol, drugs and even other criminal activity, just to get away from your judgements. We are highly over-represented in prisons and psychiatric units because of your attitude towards us, which have driven us there. The pressure of your judgements and expectations have damaged us so much that we are no longer able to feel part of society, so we form an underclass where we belong instead.

I don't even feel part of my own extended family for these exact reasons. I know the family narrative about me and i won't buy into it so i stay away. i know they won't re-write that script for me. Just one or two cousins, an aunt perhaps, are able to see beyond that script, or have ignored it, and are able to value me as i am. I wonder if they know how precious they are to me — how much i love all those who get to know me and accept me and dont patronise me with their 'effort to cope with me' but instead just open to me in acceptance, and treasure the gifts i also bring with me.

These are the true joys of ADHD, the joy of exuberance, passion, energy, relentless enthusiasm for whatever life brings next. A joyfulness that is there even if it is also crushed by you normals out there sometimes. An openness and honesty and transparency which we naturally have if we have not been too distorted and bent out of shape to express it any more by your judgements. You would get so much more from us if you stop treating us as your personal clown, an entertainment — not to be taken as human too seriously.

If our emotions appear non-existent, it is because we have frozen them to protect ourselves from your casual exasperations which amount to emotional cruelty. That often leads to trauma and possibly as in my case deep seated PTSD from childhood. Would i swap my ADHD for your lot in life.
NO.
Having observed you from the outside as it were, i do not want to be like you, it is too limiting and uninteresting to be neuro-typical. I might love you for who yo uare though anyway. It is about a mix of qualities after all.
Whatever struggles i have personally faced with this version of humanness, i have learned to appreciate it for what it is , for what it shows me in others not like us. I used to wish I coud be like them but …..It was not such a great alternative after all.
I enjoy being a little 'i'. I wear my label as a badge of honour — look what i went through to earn this — Look what I wen through to survive this, look how i survived and have deeply loving relationships still — look at the joys of having ADHD. Do you neurotypicals still jump up and down with exuberance at life some days? You are seriously missing out you know — you really are!

Oh and did my DFS, My typos and my little 'i's really bother you?

17. Socialising

'I know this is war, but the rest of us are trying to pretend it's a party.'

Kristin Cashore

Ouch! Speaking as a 'neurotypical' that last chapter was pretty bruising wasn't it? Nonetheless I read the last chapter with great interest for several reasons but let me start with one of the most striking. I believe people with ADHD are drawn to socialising despite their confusion and non-conformist social skills!

There I have said it.

Let me explain why. When Sylvia and I first met she was outgoing, involved in all sorts of things. She had travelled, she knew all sorts of people, she taught mindfulness and self-development skills, and had her first publishing contract about to manifest with her first book. Was this symptomatic of an introvert or someone who found socialising difficult? If it was then she managed to hide it very well.

One of the reasons I was drawn to her was that I was a real-life introvert who found groups of people confounding and undesirable. So how does one square this circle? What is the key to this mystery? I think it is similar to the example of ADHD people joining structured groups into which they will never fit. There is a pull towards socialising despite the inherent dangers of rejection, ridicule, and abuse because socialising opens up the possibility of new things to explore.

The other side of the coin is that ADHD people are fun, they can be outrageous, they will take the risks no one else will take, 'anyone for skinny dipping!', 'anyone for finding another night club!', 'anyone for trying out this new drug?'

They can be very popular for the very fact they are non-conformist. Interesting isn't it? Is it that there is a difference between socialising when young and when older? Possibly. Is there a difference when societal rules begin to enter into the mix? I am sure there is, dinner parties or gallery openings are a long way from raves, or the hippy gatherings of our youth are they not? It is something to consider, which is why as far as I am aware my stepson finds no difficulty socialising whereas Sylvia does, even more since her PTSD breakdown.

Those with ADHD are often intensely inquisitive and what could be better than to have the opportunity to learn about other people's lives? Socialising gives you the opportunity to do this and I have this strong feeling that the draw of interaction is stronger than the fear of not fitting in. I will sit at home content, playing guitar, reading, writing, but Sylvia is out at least three or four times week being involved with others. She runs a sangha, volunteers at the local arts centre, goes to dance class, is a chaplain at the local hospital, comes to watch my band play as part of a supportive group. I know that like the Tiger or the Killer Whale she would go mad if she couldn't be out and about doing something. So she fits into that square hole and every so often something happens and she pops out of it, then she squeezes herself back in again slightly bruised, slightly disappointed, but she does it none the less.

Speaking as a 'neurotypical' I think I ought to defend my classified group and will attempt to do so despite the fact I do fear this idea of 'them' and 'us' and to be honest I don't think it is that simple. My belief is that there are so many shades of grey between black and white it is a question of accepting we all have some of the traits of ADHD but they are less severe or they are under better control in certain people.

We can all act impulsively, we can all get into debt, we can all break the law, the majority of people have taken or take drugs (I include alcohol as the worst drug going), we can all miss appointments, forget birthdays, break rules etc., etc. And the reason I make this point is not to downgrade the problems that those diagnosed with ADHD have, it is to say 'look here is the starting point for any person to understand some of the frustration you feel'.

In order to have understanding for another, you have to have some empathy with or experience of the other.

A psychopath is never going to feel sorry for someone else's suffering because they don't have the experience or ability to understand what that means. We 'neurotypicals' can begin to understand ADHD and work with that. Let me give you a basic example, a person with ADHD makes an arrangement to meet someone, they put it in the diary just to make sure, they wake up ready for the day, they get a phone call and get distracted, they forget to look in the diary. The friend turns up and is angry that the ADHD friend hasn't bothered to keep to their arrangement. How much better would it have been if the person with ADHD said to their friend 'I will put this in the diary but would you mind giving me a call on the morning of the meeting just to jog my memory, you know what I am like and I don't want to let you down'. Wouldn't that be better? But as mentioned in previous chapters it is a two-way thing both parties need to engage in a process that enables things to work. It cannot just be a one-sided experience.

18. Living well with ADHD

Everybody is a genius but if you judge a fish by its ability to climb a tree, it will live its whole life believing it is stupid.   Albert Einstein

Typical Storytelling

With ADHD we probably do many of the same things as you NT's do but we do them differently. Like story telling as Davids diagram above suggests (based on my tendency to lose track halfway through a sentence sometimes). In fact I probably apologise about three or four more times during this process.

I used to respond on Quora and was so often approached with questions about how to live, or cope, or manage living with ADHD symptoms for daily life, or anything at all. This is tricky but not impossible.

Apart from the usual points that we all have different ADHD symptoms and challenges so there is no one cure fixes all possible, I have learned quite a lot of strategies out of necessity and desperation myself, especially in childhood, but even now in my seventh decade I am learning new ways to cope on a daily basis. If you read this as a parent try to work through it with your child instead, it may well help you both cope better.

I would say these are the main points to consider:

1. What are you predominant ADHD based deficits and positives. Perhaps even create two lists and write positive and negative aspects of all your ADHD traits and

tendencies. We are all different in exactly how they each manifest. Make sure you have fully researched all that is related to ADHD so you do not miss anything out.

2. What use can you make of each, creatively, to get the best and minimise the problems e.g. distraction — put in place as many reminders to get back on track as you are able to, and accept distractedness as a positive in some ways too — which it is — and allow yourself to be distracted up to a certain point but then recognise when it gets you into a pickle of confusion and feeling overwhelmed. I sort of develop a list of the distractions as I go through each day and try to put them into some sort of order of evaluation, usefulness and annoyance level. From there I can develop a strategy for the next day or that afternoon or whenever, to pick up and finish or prioritise — for as long as my brain allows me of course.

3. Managing the negatives so they don't become a form of self-defeat — easier said than done sometimes but even recognising I could do this made a difference to me. For instance 5 months ago I started making some curtains and a cushion for our new bedroom. Today I will finish sewing up the cushion right after I get off this chapter even though

I had intended to do that first before I looked on line again but my laptop was lying there so I picked it up and saw the chapter etc etc etc. You know the story. Recognising this means I can do something about it and not punish or get exasperated by myself at all.

4. Self-acceptance is crucial to overcoming the emotional negatives of living with ND, especially to reduce the anxiety tendencies and the all engulfing shame that can reduce one to a shivering wreck. This is how my brain is wired — this is not a judgment of me or a measure of my worth as a human. This is just a practical problem which needs practical solutions. I will get there in the end.

5. Develop mindfulness skills and also engage with the philosophy and psychology behind it, go full Buddhist without the religion, if you prefer. This really really worked for me and enabled much of what I have suggested above.

6. Measure what you do achieve rather than what you do not complete. I found that over time and with many stages, I would complete a great deal but rarely in one go — so instead of berating myself for not finishing those soft furnishings in a week — I can say with pride that I finished them all off five months later. Then I have some knitting to

complete etc. which I started a year ago. May finish before it gets warmer again — who knows?

7. Find what you can do in one go, especially if that is at work. For me it is writing which engages so much of my brain that I can finish a shorter piece off easily and am usually champing at the bit to get back to whatever my current long project is. Very hard as I have just finished another book project and promised myself a month off — but cannot stick to that. Again you get the picture if you have ADHD

8. So make rules which you can break if you want / need to. Then you do not need to punish yourself so much. We NDers tend to be very self-punishing, as if that will somehow help us to master our deficits and individual differences. It does the opposite.

9. Learn to appreciate what you have and make the most of that instead. It is worth it, and you are worth it. Self-control / management without self-punishment / shame.

19. Living Well with Someone with ADHD

'Love always cures people, both those who give it and those who receive it.'

Karl Menninger

Ok, so in the last chapter Sylvia gave a list of things people with ADHD can do to cope better. Here I will give you some ways that a person *living with someone who has ADHD* can cope better.

1. What are the negative and positive sides to your partners /child's ADHD? Write a list see what you can think of. When you have written the list ask yourself a) how can I help to alleviate the negative side of things and b) how can I make sure I tell them about the positives. As far as a) is concerned simple things like gently reminding them of things they have in the diary or need to get done. In the case of a child say to them when you get to tomorrow will you feel good for having got this done or annoyed for leaving it? Wouldn't you rather feel good than annoyed? Don't

forget to offer to do something near them if it helps, something you are getting done at the same time, this stops them feeling on their own and therefore punished. And b) look for things they have achieved, even simpler things like clearing up their dinner plates. 'Thanks for putting the dishes away.' We all like positive feedback however minor it seems.

2. Ask your partner / child 'how is it going with ……….' Not in an accusatory or judgemental way but out of genuine interest. We all like our partners to show an interest in our work / pastimes. It gives them a chance to flag up if they are ok or are having difficulties. Be genuine. If they are finding it difficult doing something, ask if there is anything you can do and be empathetic, let them know you know how it feels to struggle with certain things.

3. Don't badger them to get things done or use their difficulties against them. It doesn't help to put someone with ADHD under pressure, in fact it does the opposite, so if you really want them to finish a job, try to be as

relaxed about it as you can. I decided the curtains and the cushion Sylvia had taken five months to complete were not vital (we had blinds) so why add to Sylvia's struggle. When done they were lovely.

4. Reassure your partner /child that you understand they are doing their best when you see them struggling. Sometimes a little support goes a long way.

5. Help with the Mindfulness, try it yourself and see.

6. Be positive about their achievements when they occur. Don't say 'I like the curtains but it took you forever to make them'. You can easily cut the feet from under someone by a negative remark that achieves nothing, but satisfies your sense of superiority. Don't heap shame on them.

7. Don't expect your ADHD partner / child to be able to stick to one thing at a time. They jump from one to another without thinking and lose where they are, especially as far as time is concerned. During each distraction they become the child on the beach building

the sandcastle, totally absorbed and unable to see the waves approaching, until it is too late.

8. Try to encourage your partner / child to be forgiving to themselves whilst at the same time looking for ways to help them find loose structures they can work within (they don't do routine). For example always add half an hour on to any proposed arrival time or meeting. Try to get them to write lists when they have a number of things to do. Get a box or two where they can put paperwork etc., they won't file things but if you have one box in which they can dump paper at least they know when the time comes to find that doctors letter or that tax return it is going to be in the box and not scattered to the winds.

9. When you are about to criticise think of support, praise or encouragement instead.

20. PTSD, ADHD and its Complications

'The human body experiences a powerful gravitational pull in the direction of hope. That is why the patient's hope is the physicians secret weapon' Norman Cousins

I was diagnosed with ADHD in my mid-fifties and my relief was palpable. Finally I had an explanation for so much in my life and I could stop beating myself up for apparently being so deficient on so many planes that even my own parents found me unconscionable.

It wasn't a deficiency in my personality after all, I couldn't help it.

I had spent most of my life being ashamed of existing anyway, thanks to my parents approach to parenting and relationships. They certainly brought out the worst in each other. And they focused on my deficiencies most of all, as a way of avoiding examining their own, I guess. Certainly self-reflection wasn't in their game plan any time I remember. Thus I also developed PTSD, probably from about three years old.

However living with these differences still rears its more ugly head from time to time. People put me into pressure cooker situations and I blow. Then they stand back and blame me for my response. I am supposed to accommodate their needs but not them to accommodate mine. That is so similar to my childhood abuse set up that is also triggers my PTSD remnants. Apparently that is still my lack of self-mastery, not their lack of awareness, insight or sensitivity. ADHD can lead to emotional volatility, so can being Aries and so can PTSD triggers. I might just be up against enormous odds.

For example someone who had hurt me badly but pretended it wasn't them came up to me very smugly and put their hand on my arm, I turned on them.

'Don't touch me, don't dare touch me.'

I then went on to remind them of the decision they'd made which really did re-traumatise me pretty badly, the effects of which lasted for two years and still lingers inside myself. I am not supposed to know who it was, but it isn't rocket science to guess, and I am pretty intuitive, so roughly 95% certain I am right. It was a bit of a tirade, but not unjustified.

So am I ashamed of my behaviour?

No.

I am quite chuffed actually.

As an abused child I could never have spoken out to defend myself from unwanted anything and got away with it. You learn pretty soon that sticking up for yourself with abusive parents just makes it worse for you. I learned how to freeze everything so I felt nothing, instead. Learning how to unfreeze myself once more took decades and a complete breakdown, which was living hell, but which ultimately liberated me from my emotional defence prisons, and left me very open and raw and vulnerable. I like being open and work hard not to close it down again defensively, but it takes a toll in its own way too

I write a lot about mindfulness and practice and teach it as much as I can. Was my spontaneous outburst showing my lack of mindfulness skill? Well of course this other person will almost certainly think it is so. That would be their defence against their own complicity and ill-considered unkindness in singling me out in the first place. Also I doubt that their had considered that putting their hands onto someone without their permission is actually a power negotiation.

I don't enjoy the fact that I reacted so strongly, but it happened before I had a chance to know how I would react. I accept it. I mostly respond fairly skilfully to situations nowadays but no one knows how they will respond or react under extreme stress.

Believe me this was a pretty extreme source of distress for me as situations go.

Physical contact is a powerful communication and it can be about control and power, (witness the handshaking games played by and with Trump in his early presidency) which I had previously experienced with this person anyway. But physical contact, when used lovingly, can be extremely healing, as I have written about in the past. This touch was not a healing one. It had no humility or tenderness in it for me. Instead it had attention seeking and dominance, assumption of rights and superiority, probably completely unrecognised by herself. My body read this and reacted before I knew what was happening. That is trauma.

The mindfulness approach I am now taking with myself is one of acceptance and forgiveness. Letting go of emotional burdens through forgiveness allows you to be more present and settled into this present moment. I am pretty much there more often than not nowadays.

I totally emotionally forgive those people who hurt me but my body is still reacting defensively at cellular level. It doesn't want them near me. That is what trauma does, it rewires the defence systems to trigger sensitive. You just do not have time to get in between the event and the defence response. I can now recognise that this is a positive step forward for me and I will work with this consciously and lovingly. Yes now I am able to stick up for myself and defend myself, but do I need to still? Is that the best way for me as an adult of 69 yrs old? I don't think so.

As someone who has really struggled daily through life with PTSD, ADHD and being very highly sensitive / psychic/ intuitive/ empathic, I experience life in the acute lane. I have too many mirror neurons for my own good. But I do a great deal for many people and give of my best whenever I am able. I also take care of myself and tend to live a pretty reclusive lifestyle unless I am 'doing something'. Even then I prefer not to have too many people around me and avoid large social situations as much as I can.

SO my ADHD / PTSD based deficiencies!

These are deficiencies mostly pointed out to me by other people, not issues I personally have with how I cope with life nowadays. I am actually incredibly happy in my own life and love every minute of it. I have no regrets and no bitterness. I am how I am, and I have more or less total acceptance for myself nowadays, which is something of a huge achievement.

My only problem in life is public ignorance of mental health and/or cognitive disability issues and how much harder it is for people with PTSD, ADHD or any other string of initials we are given as labels, as a result. The projected struggle given to us on top of our own struggles is an enormous burden, one we have to face on a daily basis.

On top of developing our alternative cognitive skills in ways that are necessary to work with ADHD and manage the expectations of normal people, we have to fit into a society not designed for us.

Neuro-typical society and the way it is designed is actually the disabling factor, not our brains.

There are so many great things about having ADHD which I have written about elsewhere. I wouldn't want to be anyone else, and if I was, I wouldn't have such great family/ husband and friends, all of whom accept me for exactly how I am, complexities and all.

21. Sylvia Clare ADHD PTSD

'Awards can give you a tremendous amount of encouragement to keep getting better, no matter how young or old you are.' Alan Alder

Sylvia stands on the podium clasping her Golden Brain award for lifetime achievement. 'I would like to thank you all for this recognition that I have lived with ADHD & PTSD the whole of my life. I would like to thank my husband, my family, Jon Kabat Zinn, Thich Nhat Hanh, Joni Mitchell and Isabel Allende, for getting me through this traumatic experience. Without their support I might not have survived.'

OK so a diagnosis of ADHD or PTSD isn't quite the same as the Oscars but in a way it can be a very positive recognition that the diagnosed person has an actual medical condition and should be acknowledged as someone who is doing their best despite considerable odds stacked against them. Certainly to Sylvia it was as good as an award as she explained in the last chapter. At last someone recognised there was something different about the way she thought and therefore behaved. At last she wasn't 'getting it wrong', she was getting it as right as she could, given the cards she had been dealt. She was vindicated.

I remember her joy at receiving the news and the news about her son, it was that Oscar nomination moment.

At the time I don't think I understood just how much it meant to her nor what it would mean for the future. As I have explained earlier in the book, I was not up on all of these medical abbreviations, or the reasons for them, and I had my suspicions about them. There is always a double-edged sword to such things. On the one hand the recognition of a problem and on the other a sort of brand that you carry with you and by which you are judged.

On a personal level for someone like Sylvia it is a tremendous boost to know why you don't quite function as the majority do. On a wider note I do have a problem with the issues around labels and whether they are beneficial, and I would like to talk a little more about this in a moment.

I also worry about the fact the way it seems to work is that whenever there is a clinically recognised condition there is a pharmaceutical company ready to suppress it. There is big big money in ADHD drugs and prescribing them. It is very worrying how much is prescribed and how little is known of the long-term effects of these drugs. I also find it disturbing that drugs are the first port of call rather than other forms of support such as education, and techniques such as Mindfulness. At this point some readers may say 'well you would promote Mindfulness wouldn't you?' The answer to that is 'Yes I would' because it has been shown to help. It is not 'the answer' but neither are prescription or street drugs!

So back to labels. Earlier in the book Sylvia referred to someone who suggested she mentioned her ADHD and PTSD a bit too much. I suppose the question is, when is it appropriate or useful to mention such things? This is such a difficult thing to answer but I will give it a try. Let's start with a different scenario that might help illustrate the point.

'You've made me itchy'

'Oh….didn't I tell you I've got Chlamydia'

There are times when it just might help to tell someone something before you engage in a mutual project. Going back to the work situation it might help to tell someone you have ADHD if they insist on you single handedly planning and executing a society wedding for someone in a short timescale and on a small budget. But whether it is appropriate to randomly say to someone standing in the checkout queue 'I've got ADHD you know' is another matter. So it is context as much as anything.

Some people don't like labels no matter what. They don't like Feminists, Bikers, Twitchers, LGBT 'ers, etc., etc. It immediately puts their back up because they don't want to be confronted by someone 'different'. It is too much hard work and anyway 'why do they think they are so special'. What is the point in telling them you have ADHD, PTSD, Dyslexia, Dyspraxia etc., etc? None whatsoever and yet they may be the very people who you want to get through to! Forget it. Their argument is that they think people classify themselves as one or other thing in order to be treated differently and therefore get some advantage. In the case of ADHD, 'oh your child is allowed to behave badly are they, because they have ADHD?'

It has to be accepted that often telling someone you have a diagnosis is not going to help.

There is also the fatigue factor that comes into play, what one might call Fanatical Vegan Syndrome or FVS. Ok so you are a Vegan but unless you are ordering your meal I don't need to know. Otherwise it becomes a bit like that Monty Python sketch of the Spanish Inquisition where no matter where you are or what you are doing someone springs out at you and in this case tells you they have this or that condition. It can be dangerous too for someone to identify as their diagnosis. 'I can't do that because I am.......' It limits them and it limits how other people see them too.

At the end of the day it is important for people to receive a diagnosis to help them understand themselves but whether telling someone you have a certain diagnosis helps them to understand you is dependent on their need to know and their willingness to listen. If you have to explain it to everyone, come what may, then FVS syndrome kicks in. Don't tell me unless you are ordering your meal. Obviously if you pick up a book such as this you expect to hear the term ADHD used a lot, if you pick up a book about gardening then you don't. Context again.

So to those who have ADHD, FVS, LGBT, MBE's, DFC's, Master of the Rolls etc., use your handles carefully and only when you really need to. If someone wants to know then they will ask you, if someone needs to know then you can tell them.

22. Loving yourself with ADHD

'To love oneself is the start of a lifelong affair.' Oscar Wilde

I love having ADHD nowadays.

It was not always like that.

How can we love ourselves when we are so much of a problem to everyone else?

What would I like to tell my younger self now about how to live, or cope, or manage living with ADHD symptoms for daily life, or anything at all.

This is tricky but not impossible. ADHD is a great challenge to take on.

All humans are utterly unique, yet our similarities far outweigh our differences and that is something to bear in mind always, in all areas of human life.

People with ADHD all have different ADHD symptoms and challenges so there is no 'one cure fixes all' possible, though meds do try to suggest that sometimes. I had to stop taking them, the positives were there but they messed with my brain too much. Some people find they help a great deal - we are all individuals. I wasn't offered alternatives to try though I have learned quite a lot of strategies out of necessity and desperation myself, especially in childhood, but even now in my seventh decade I am learning new ways to cope on a daily basis. I also wish I had known much of this when I had my two sons, who also both have ADHD symptoms. My younger son and I get through more easily because we both have high IQ's which is a massive help in terms of self-regulation and finding ways of coping. My eldest son is intelligent, but not quite as highly. He had massive sleep deprivation in his early infancy, and has struggled more as a result. We are all different, it is not a competition. He is now settled in his life though and happily, if chaotically, organising his own circumstances as well as anybody. We all found ways of living and earning money that worked for us and at which we could excel. I know of other people with ADHD who have found similar but also several who have not. However it took us all quite a lot more time and this is OK too.

I raised two sons, much of it as a single mum, and having ADHD myself, I thus spent incredible amounts of time and energy, and much of my adult life, trying to find ways to suppress and coerce them and myself into conformity. I ultimately failed us all. I now see clearly the error of my ways and also how different things might have been for us all if I had understood then what I understand now. We all made it through our lives thus far more or less well as can be expected but it has been painful for us. If this book can shift a few attitudes and beliefs to make that less of a struggle for others in the future then we shall have achieved some greater good.

Why I do love my ADHD

Living with ADHD can be a real drag at times. I often feel like I have to explain or justify myself so that others don't 'get me wrong'. That basically means not judging, overlooking and/ or dismissing me in so many ways, as has happened throughout my life. The few that don't do that are my most treasured friends and some family members too, and they mean the absolute world to me.
BUT
ADHD makes you endlessly restless, your brain whirring with more ideas than you can reasonably cope with. There are lots of

ways this is expressed. In my life, it makes me exhaustively curious, fascinated by the amazing nature of lived experiences. I am excited by the endless spectacular qualities of the natural world. There is so much to explore and observe, to enjoy and learn from on a daily basis. Life is just so alive with amazing things.

The restlessness is useful. It allows me to do all the things that fascinate me. My list of regular, if not completely daily, activities is a long one. I do / am a bee-keeper, a gardener and grower of vegetables, a pickler, fermenter and preserver, a cold sea swimmer, a walker and forager, a writer and poet, a storyteller, a thinker, an avid reader, a teacher, an organiser, a lover/wife and mother, a good friend, a musicians wife and assistant roadie, a friend, a curtain maker, a knitter, a hospital chaplaincy assistant until recently, a grandmother, a sangha leader, a quaker, a buddhist philosophy student, and a few more, in no particular order.

The energy, enthusiasm, curiosity and fascination are still as a young child's might be, never having really left me, just calmed down a little. I could never be a conventional wife and mother, but I did both and am doing OK and so are my sons and second husband, just not conventionally.

I remember once when my sons were little, about 3 & 5 and it was a hot summer. They were in a cool bath getting ready to go to bed. They kept splashing me. I was trying to stop them but laughing too much and simultaneously worrying about the ceiling below the bathroom. I didn't feel in the mood for a confrontation with them or to spoil the fun time they were having for good, but to them, boring reasons.

So I just got into the bath with them, fully dressed but minus sandals, and said now you can splash me all you like. They did. I had to strip off before I could get out again, but it was such fun to play with them like that instead of getting serious. Would someone without ADHD have done that? I don't know. Perhaps, but it is just one example of why staying playful as a result of your ADHD is worth putting up with the down sides for.

Would I stop being ADHD to be normal?

Never, on my life! I wouldn't cope with the boredom

BUT ALL THREE OF US found that one of the hardest things to cope with was the judgments and expectations of other people and their ignorance of what it is reasonable to expect of us.

This applied to extended family as well, their need to judge us and look down on us. It was a toxic culture.

I have a favourite saying:-

'WHATEVER YOUR EXPECTATIONS OF ME, I'M SURE TO DISAPPOINT YOU'.

That saying is based wholly on living with my parent's words perpetually ringing in my ears, 'if it wasn't for you the whole family would be happy'.

There is a lot of damaged psychology behind that comment and I have since learned to read it in a different way, but I am talking about growing up with un-diagnosed ADHD and PTSD, and how that affected me then.

Teachers and extended family all seemed to join in too. There really was no respite. All schools said I was lazy, didn't concentrate and was a disappointment. Teachers often bullied me to try harder (they had no idea!) and used sarcasm to make me achieve what they thought I should achieve but never offered me any help to get there. Apart from the very occasional one or two who did, and it worked wonders for me. I am eternally grateful to Mrs Shoebridge for maths and Mrs Waters for english. You have no idea.

Whether you read this as a parent or as an individual trying to heal your own ADHD related wounds of self-worth, try to work through it in stages, and with your child or partner if relevant. It may well help you both cope better.

First of all educate yourself about ADHD, and ND, in all its various manifestations.

So to begin:

Work out where you are on the ND spectrum.

What are you predominant ADHD based deficits and positives including all the secondary ones, not just hyperactivity and inattention.

Create two lists and write positive and negative aspects of all your ADHD traits and tendencies. We are all different in exactly how they each manifest.

Be creative in how you positively view your ADHD — my husband often says how he loves that he will never be bored living with me and he loves the challenges.

Look at everything from different angles and see how creative you can make your positives, even if this is not happening at the moment. This is a very important step to take.

What use can you make of each common ADHD trait, creatively, to get the best and minimise the problems. Here are some examples:

Distraction — put in place as many reminders to get back on track as you are able to,

Accept distractedness as a positive in some ways too — which it is — and allow yourself to be distracted up to a certain point — for me it stops boredom and allows me to come back fresh to a task every time, when I get around to it. It also means I can respond instantly and positively to sudden demands and necessities. I am responsive and flexible when necessary. Recognise when it gets you into a pickle of confusion and feeling overwhelmed. Develop strategies to reduce this self-punishing style.

Work out how you might be able to manage that activity differently, creatively and lovingly.

I try to have a few things that I know I will complete that day and then allow myself to flit from one thing to another later on, knowing that over several days I will have done enough flitting to complete them all, one way or another.

Manage the negatives so they don't become a form of self-defeat — easier said than done sometimes but even recognising I could do this made a difference to me.

Don't beat yourself up for them. Sometimes taking distraction breaks whilst working towards completing a task means you get different perspectives on it. That can be really helpful too.

Allow these differences to be what they are and notice how they give you alternatives from a neuro-typical person.

Self acceptance and loving your differences is crucial to overcoming the emotional negatives of living with ADHD, especially to reduce the anxiety tendencies.

Remember — say to yourself — 'this is how my brain is wired, this is not a judgment of me or a measure of my worth as a human. This is just a practical problem which needs practical solutions. I will get there in the end'.

Amongst other things Mindfulness helped turn everything around for me. It helped me go from subconsciously as worthless as a beaten dog to celebrating my ADHD-ness. That took time but it was the principal influence, along with a husband who loves me more for my ADHD-ness, and supports me in managing it rather than using it as a weapon to put me down with.

This really really worked for me and enabled much of what I have suggested above. It is why I am now writing full-time pretty much, have many books published and many more underway.

Whoever would have though it eh????

Measure what you do achieve

Count the positives rather than what you do not complete. I found that over time and with many stages or attempts, I would complete a great deal but rarely in one go.

Instead of berating myself for not finishing those soft furnishings in a week — I can say with pride that I finished them all off today, five months after starting them. Or that flower bed that I started weeding last week. I finished that this afternoon. (I will do — probably — once I have done all the other things on my list of priorities and if I don't get distracted too much elsewhere and as long as the phone doesn't ring or the bees don't swarm on me again).

Find what you can do in one go, especially if that is at work. For me it is writing which engages so much of my brain that I can finish a shorter piece off easily and am usually champing at the bit to get back to whatever my current long project is. Gardening too , I can never get enough gardening time.

Make rules or guidelines to help yourself and know which you can break if you want / need to, and which preferably not. Then you do not need to punish yourself so much. We ADHD ers tend to be very self-punishing, as if that will somehow help us to master our deficits and individual differences. It doesn't of course — it just burdens us with even more self-doubt and low self-worth.

Learn to appreciate what you have with your ADHD.

My Positives are:-

Exuberance and a childlike thrill about life on good days.

Over time I get an enormous amount done.

I can hyperfocus on certain projects for quite a long and intensive time and then need to burn off the physical steam which has built up by going for fast walks or doing a hundred jumping jacks in my kitchen (at 64).

I am never boring but I am very spontaneous and affectionate with people who value me fully and for them I am a very loving and loyal friend.

I am compassionate — I understand suffering, mental illness and much more.

So please find a way to enjoy your ADHD-ness and make the most of that instead of seeing it as a disability or a problem. It is worth it, and you are worth it.

23. Loving someone with ADHD

'I would not want to belong to a club that would have me as a member.' Groucho Marx

There was a moment when I realised I had a choice. I didn't like the discarded wrapping paper and boxes left in the wake of Sylvia's distracted comings and goings. I didn't like hearing that she had missed yet another appointment and was cross with herself for letting someone else down. I didn't like making her a meal only to find she had wandered down the garden just before it was dished up and was planting something. I didn't like opening the credit card envelope to find that despite the fact we had agreed not to spend there was something else on the list. I didn't like the constant need to be somewhere else, to do something else, to create something else.

That's a lot of 'didn't like(s)' isn't it? So what did I like? Well actually I liked all of those things except I didn't know it at the time. Confusing eh? Tell me about it. I loved this woman who did all of these things I 'didn't like'.

How does that work?

The answer is simple and yet incredible.

She does all of the things I would not allow myself to do. Take a moment to absorb that one. Instead of 'didn't like' read 'you mustn't.'

Although Sylvia would dispute this, I do endeavour to be tidy. I am a stickler for punctuality. I always feel dreadful if I am late for an appointment, and heaven forbid I should actually miss one. I always kept an eye on the money (my father's austere teaching). I won't go on but you get the picture. She did all of the things I was taught not to do. For example in my father's household you were never late to the dinner table or you didn't eat.

The irony in all of this and the crux of the matter was that I did not actually like being who I was but I didn't know it. If I was 'neurotypical' then it was because I had been taught to be 'neurotypical' whilst growing up, but I didn't like it (notice another 'didn't like' - I am good at those) but I didn't know how to be different.

So there was this huge conflict when living with Sylvia. There she was appearing to not care and doing what she wanted (when in fact she couldn't do anything else) and there was me with my 'didn't like(s)' who wished I could do the things she did and yet get away with it.

You could say it was a sort of weird parallel universe going on, 'how come she can get away with it and I can't' 'how come he always gets it right and I don't'.

Both of us were trapped, she by her neural wiring and me by a rigid upbringing that said 'this is how things must be'.

Thank goodness for that unknowable thing called love that held things together whilst we battered our brains out trying to suss it all. Of course we didn't 'suss it all' but what happened was this. For my part, I made a logical decision based on the following argument :-

I love her, yet she drives me mad. I have a choice. I can stick with her and bombard her with 'don't likes' and try to change her, in which case she won't actually be the person I fell in love with anymore and I will feel really mean for constantly picking on her, or I can say 'ok I will accept everything she does without judgement and see what happens.'

What was remarkable was that a great weight was lifted from my shoulders. My love for Sylvia increased and I began to give myself the freedom to do some of the things I had been taught I shouldn't. I bought more than one book at a time. I became more honest both with myself and others, and I began to say 'no I don't want to do that' if I didn't feel like doing something. I loosened up.

Allowing Sylvia to be who she was without judgement gave me the freedom to find myself.

It is all a bit Walt Disney isn't it? Well not really because of course I still managed to judge some of her behaviour until my approach became embedded and let's not forget <u>she still found me remarkably frustrating</u> in my neurotypical way but at least we were both able to work at this idea that we were <u>both</u> doing our best.

It was not one sided.

One of the things ADHD people really dislike is that they are responsible for putting things right, it is all down to them to change. Now we both had to. For us a new form of understanding emerged that has led us to where we are and that place is good. Nowadays it is actually a bit Disney, but I won't gloat, it was hard won <u>by both of us</u>.

24. Enjoying life after Diagnosis

'If growing up means it is beneath my dignity to climb a tree, I'll never grow up, never grow up, never grow up!' J.M. Barrie

My brain is like an arcade game always playing at full volume in my head. It is noisy, distracting, exhausting and endlessly confusing. It is also exhilarating, entertaining and creative, funny, enthusiastic and there is some part of me that loves it.
I also still like climbing trees
But it was not always like that.
I always knew I was different.
I thought my parents were right, it was all me and if I didn't exist everyone would be much better off.
The teachers at school seemed to imply they felt the same way too.
 And it didn't matter how hard I worked at getting it right, I just couldn't.
 There was something wrong with how my brain worked and everything in life just seemed impossible.

ADHD wasn't really understood or thought about in the 1950's–1980's, even though it was first identified in 1902 by George Frederic Still who described it as a moral control defect in some children who were nevertheless still intelligent. In 1922 Alfred Tredgold, a leading brain impairment at the time, identified the behaviours as brain impairment and not bad behaviours. In 1937 a doctor, Charles Bradley, found that giving his child patients benzedrine for headaches helped their performance and interest levels, and thus started the medical model of ADHD as something to cure. In 1971 Dr Paul Wender noticed how ADHD tended to run in families, introducing the suggestion of inherited or genetic links. Up until 1980 it was called hyperkinetic disorder but now it is called ADHD in the DSM third edition. Since then there have been similar stages in appreciating that it is not only children, that medication does work for some over long periods of life and it is a real thing. It is not something invented to make drug companies rich.

I have written earlier about my struggles with PTSD as a result of my parents attempts to punish me out of having ADHD. They just made it worse. Life growing up was not easy. I stumbled from one crisis to another, using a spiritual journey paradigm to hold myself together (I believe this is real and helps everyone who chooses it).

I had a PTSD based breakdown crisis which proved to be a complete and genuine turning point in my life. It cleared out all or most of the emotional debris in one brutal emotional tidal wave, during which my husband held me both tightly and lightly, keeping me safe and giving me gentle sanctuary whilst the storm raged through my being, trusting always that I would come through and we would still be together, which we are. The universe wanted me to survive for some reason, so they put us together, because I am very sure I would not have made it out alive or in any sane functional form without him. I don't believe anyone else alive could have helped me in this way.

But when I was healing, I realised I still had these symptoms or 'behaviour patterns' which matched my sons, who had by then been properly diagnosed with ADHD. I struggled to find a doctor who would give me a diagnosis, they all just said it was still PTSD, but I could feel the differences in these symptoms, I could discern the PTSD remnants and that they were qualitatively different to the other ones. Eventually my husband was also convinced I had ADHD as it made sense of much of my personality/ behaviour traits.

Finally I found a psychiatrist who would listen to someone in their late fifties with no school reports or family alive who could confirm what I was like as a child, but who was prepared to believe me and my husband as we told him what I was like.
I got the diagnosis and it changed my life.
Not because I had meds to take to help me cope with it. I did take concerta for a while but then stopped them, and preferred to cope using my mindfulness, but because I now understood why I was the way I was and it wasn't MY FAULT.
The Diagnosis gave me back my sense of goodness, lovability, acceptability and a reason why it wasn't something I could help. It allowed me to relax and enjoy life instead of struggling to fight against my ADHD. It allowed me to embrace my ND nature and work with it instead of against it. I have already written about its positives, but my ADHD is now a valuable part of my marriage and my creative life, not a disability but a difference that gives me/ us challenges, but also advantages if I choose to harness them.
It doesn't take away the areas I struggle with, but my adorable husband is very appreciative and supportive and we work together to each other's strengths and weaknesses. The mutual

support means there is no judgement or criticism for my ADHD nature.

We are now using the insight to support my eldest son who is also an adult but who still struggles greatly with many of the ADHD related issues, but our insight and compassion helps him get through and achieve, even if it takes him longer to get there. We also love him for his ADHD and well as acknowledge the challenges it confronts him with for living independently, but he got there, is doing well and we adore him for it.

Life with ADHD as an adult is interesting. Nowadays it is never boring or routine, it is full of love and laughter and slight madness, which makes it a much more exhilarating adventure. My husband says he will never be bored with me, never fall into any kind of rut or complacency, and never get too old for adventures. It is nice to be appreciated for being disabled or differently-abled — finally.

25. ADHD saved my Life - Possibly

Life has always been an uphill struggle for me.

I expect that is true of many people with neurodiversity, that what others take for granted we struggle with, the proverbial swan smoothly gliding and paddling furiously beneath the surface.

It was after my diagnosis in my mid-fifties that I started to explore ADHD in more depth though, and realised how much it had done for me as well as made life more difficult.

ADHD makes you tend towards being bouncy, whether you feel like it or not sometimes too. It can also make you feel very low and depressed by the frustration of the struggle to come close to anything considered normal. This means we can often feel like failures, but we're not. The fact that we struggle makes us amazing, survivors, people who don't give up, who have great perseverance and who are always looking to better themselves.

This is the exact opposite of those who are complacent and do little or nothing to work on themselves. Being normal comes easily to them and they think they have it sorted out. But they don't either, in almost all cases.

Let me get back to the bouncy part though. I have also struggled with complex trauma and PTSD since early childhood. As I said life has been challenging. eras my parents thought they could punish and shame the ADHD out of me when all they did was add to it. But I endured and found ways to have a happy life in between the bouts of depression, and I put this down to the enthusiasm and general bouncy nature of my ADHD.

ADHD has given me these positive qualities

Endless curiosity which leads to impulsiveness, which leads to all sorts of mad adventures and projects, some of which come out triumphant and some of which flop impressively too. But they stop me being down on myself too much, well maybe not the failures, but then I'm immediately off chasing something new. That is very ADHD and can be very healing and restorative after a bad bout of self doubt and self punishment.

A lack of focus on past or future and a full engagement with the present. Now is all that matters. It can lead to a need for instant gratification but my mindfulness practice has taken care of that and I find I can stay present quite easily for much of the time. It is the distractability of ADHD which makes anything instantly compelling in this moment and can pull me into something new and away from the darkness which does gather around me

An inappropriate sense of humour which allows me to laugh at myself in spite of my difficulties—witness my self-label 'old wobbly feelings thingy twithead'. See what I mean? Who can get down with that hanging above your head on the headboard of your bed, (my husband put it there to make me laugh in a particularly difficult few days)? He would also give me lots of cuddles and re-assurance when I was particularly down on myself.

hyperactivity has always been a challenge, not being able to sit and watch tv even without having to get up or have something else to do with my hands and sometimes my mind too. Knitting is my go-to with this but hyperactivity itself is a positive. It means I am on the go and thus creating lots of positive energy vibes for myself from aerobic activity. It also keeps me fairly fit, and productive in my garden and vegetables growing, in my love for swimming and dancing, and my enjoyment of moderately long-distance walking, although that is getting harder now I have arthritis developing in many joints.

Having a mindfulness practice enabled me to recognise all these positives from being neurodivergent, and allowed me to embrace and accept it as just how I am and not deficit issues after all.

As I go towards the end of my seventh decade of life, I am still active and doing masses of things, sometimes too much and I get overwhelmed, but I am getting better at not letting that happen, and am very dependent on my diary to remind me of what I must do each day. Mindfulness also allows me to reset myself several times a day with a few breaths and a general letting go and re-centering process which allows me to keep the excesses of ADHD under some control too.

I am intelligent and although I find it hard to maintain concentration over long periods of time, I do absorb information that interests me like a sponge—still- after all these years I am always looking for books that give me new insights into life itself, this planet and its inhabitants. I am very aware of how insignificant we are individually or even as a species other than our ability to destroy all that is around us. This has led me towards being far more conscious and aware of the importance of how we live our lives, with the awareness of all others, of being environmentally aware and considerate to all others as much as we are able to be. Without ADHD I may have Sunk into complacency and lack of interest in endless searching out the new in my life, like so many people have done, just plodding through life and avoiding too much in the way of discomfort and challenge. Yet it is through these challenging experiences that we grow.

Do I want to not have ADHD and the possible bit of autism my husband thinks I also may have? No! Not on your nelly. But it is time we helped people with neuro-divergency feel valued in society, and taught mindfulness as a way of looking at life from early childhood onwards. That way I might have avoided the PTSD. But even the darkness has some value sometimes. Without mindfulness as a lens through which I could learn to accept and value myself and not denigrate myself as my parents and teachers did when I was growing up, life might have been a little easier at times, but who knows which lessons I might not have learned.

And without the ADHD I am sure the trauma, which would have been there anyway, would have killed me, defeated me, destroyed me. So yes I conclude my ADHD saved my life. Interesting isn't it, when you take a look at your own life through a different lens, reframe it, explore the what-ifs and spin it with a positive lens.

26. Where do we go from here?

'Travel is fatal to bigotry and narrow mindedness, and many people need it sorely on this account.' Mark Twain

Despite loving to travel, Sylvia and I have decided that air travel and the continuance of the planet do not go together. It is with regret that we are not going to the Arctic, the Antarctic, to Japan, to Chile, to……well anywhere we haven't been. You come to realisations, mostly later in life, that you have been covertly ignoring all the things you know to be right, justifying your actions by saying 'it's just this once' or 'it's only me, what does it matter?'

So why the Mark Twain quote inviting you to travel to overcome bigotry and narrow mindedness?

Well there is travelling and there is travelling. I would suggest that there are a great many people who are stuck in one place in their mind. Their experience is of being comfortable surrounded by like-minded, similarly schooled individuals who like myself had been trained to think along narrow lines. This is what you do, this is what you don't do, these are the consequences for not conforming.

Now to someone with ADHD the consequences don't really influence them in the same way, at least not in the way they would the 'ordinary' person. They do things, then face whatever comes after.

What is it that you find fascinating about going abroad? Everything is slightly different isn't it? People do things differently, they dress differently, they eat differently, they even go to sleep in the afternoon.

We love it.

How exciting to be amongst such different people. There is often an element of risk. Can we trust the taxi driver not to kill us with his driving, can we rely on the guide to get us there, do we have enough money to do this thing or that? We even go bungee jumping, hot air ballooning, climbing mountains and swimming in rain forest pools. Often there is an element of discomfort, the bed is too hard, the donkey too small, the aircraft too rickety. But we love it. It is exciting. We overspend, we get to the airport at the last minute, we buy things we don't really want or need, but it is really good fun. We have stories to tell, experiences we don't normally have, we are not bored. Ring any bells?

All of the above and more I have found in Sylvia as a person. I travelled with her around her ADHD world and accepted the ups and downs. I accepted the differences, the last minute dashes, the empty wallets, the hair raising moments when I thought we were both doomed. It has been an incredible journey, taking me out of myself and shaking me out of my complacency, my righteous indignation, my pomposity. Thank you Sylvia and thank you for your ADHD, you have made me a better man.

Monkey mind

Calm the mind,

focus on breath.

I will when I have

finished swinging

in this tree over here.

Fully present and joyful.

Oh wait no I must attend

to this also, imperative.

And then 'this breath, this moment,

it is all that exists.'

The ever constant now

fully present with love.

The past and future,

hard to consider, dwell in shadow.

But the present, the amazing present moment,

so full and alive with everything.

No filters on an ADHD monkey brain

I swing gloriously through each tree in the forest,

exploring it all,

fully present and aware.

Who wants a stilled mind

when there is so much life

right here right now?

Fully present and alive.

So much joy and simple happiness.

A monkey mind on steroids.

Fully present and awake,

not missing a thing.

27. How do people with ADHD find their futures?

Are you a parent with a school leaver coming up? Do they have cognitive neuro-divergency — or perhaps not? Are they just non-conformists? There are no easy answers but there are ways of exploring the question.

So often at school those with cognitive neurodiversity issues are left feeling there is nothing they are much good at. This is so very, very, wrong. People who do not fit into convenient boxes are so often alienated from the rest of life.

It is one of the huge failings of our academic system, that it caters for such a narrow band of people in life, and in the process ignores vast oceans of potential that could seriously benefit humankind in many more imaginative ways. But most people are channelled into employment fodder roles for those who 'create jobs' so that they can make themselves rich from the effort of others. Many of these roles are relatively impossible for people with ADHD, if not downright abusive. We need lots of variety, stimulation and usually a fair bit of physical activity thrown in to burn off our excessive energy. We also need to play to our own individual strengths as it is more or less impossible to force someone with ADHD into the wrong shaped hole. They can be amazingly great, but they cannot shape shift so easily. Actually this is true or all people to some extent, but we are just a little more like that.

So these are the kinds of questions we need to be asking young people who are thinking about their future. The other people who need to consider these questions are parents, carers and all those involved with teaching and offering skills for life to these youngsters too. Otherwise we undermine them before they can even get started.

What are your strengths?

What are you good at?

People with ADHD often say nothing because that is how they have been made to feel, especially in school. But can they make people laugh, can they be fun, do they show artistic skills or interesting ways of looking at life.

No one has nothing they are good at.

Then what excites you, what are you drawn towards that is positive in life.

Make a list of reasons you consider might make your future more engaging, part of your challenge to do something different.

Life is not supposed to be too easy — we grow through challenges and find out who we are through struggle.

We once taught mindfulness to a wonderful sculptor who made amazing sculptures out of scrap metal — stunning they were. He had the same list - ADHD, Dyslexia and some social shyness. He worked alone but was married.

My list is ADHD, PTSD, social anxiety, and yet I managed to find a life as a writer and mindfulness teacher, after trying teaching academia. But I had to get out of that when they turned it into accountancy exercises rather than sharing a love of your chosen subject.

I also am a beekeeper and a gardener, and a parent and now grandparent. The latter two are more roles in life. Both beekeeping and gardening feed my need for nature and physical activity and masses of variety. They are all possibilities for full time or money earning options. I like having several income streams instead of just the one anyway, but I work for myself not others nowadays.

Some of our best comics and people in the arts generally are also introverts and have ADHD or distinct traits of it. Think of Robin Williams, Sue Perkins, Lee Mack, Jim Carey, Whoopie Goldberg and many many more. The comedian Rory Bremner shared his heart breaking struggle with ADHD on air in this documentary BBC Two — Horizon, 2017, ADHD and Me with Rory Bremner, What's it like to be inside Rory Bremner's brain? . Yet he is such a successful adult in his own life in so many other ways.

And this clip shows how hard it can be to concentrate BBC Two — Horizon, 2017, ADHD and Me with Rory Bremner, Trail — ADHD and Me with Rory Bremner

One of the best qualities many people with ADHD have is to think outside the box. Try brainstorming a few of the things you do like and see where it takes you. This is one of the observations made in this documentary.

So how do you guide young people where to go in their future life?

Try asking questions of them / yourself. Which do you prefer best — indoors or outdoors, active or sedentary, with people or not with other people i.e. do they distract you or help you stay on task.

Though I am able to mix those sets of contradictions up, not everyone can do this successfully.

But I have found myself being hounded out of jobs due to changes in policy that made it impossible for people with

ADHD. I also know I would not have been any good at all in jobs that required a great deal of discretion and tact – like funeral directors. I loved teaching when it was about inspiring young people but had to leave when it turned into accountancy exercises. Instead I just teach mindfulness now. Exactly up my street.

I had to stop thinking about jobs as such, career paths and destinies and learn to respond to life as it evolved around me and think about situations where I felt better. I had to find my own places of power and move towards them even though they put me in all sorts of conflicted situations.

Another thing is to look at skills that seem to be specific or enhanced in people with ADHD. Can you hyperfocus? I was able to use this faculty of mine to write about things that interested me, but I was equally useless in writing academic papers etc as that was dry and uninspiring so even though my IQ suggested I should walk a PhD, I just couldn't manage to express that in a way that academia would value. I struggled through my MSc. in research psychology and my MA in creative writing. Academia and I are certainly not happy bedfellows and most people with ADHD would not even bother.

My sons are able to hyperfocus on computer games and both thought about being games testers — they are both ADHD/dyslexic too but they ended up going into very different lines of work. Building has called to one of them, or rather that is where he ended up as he also liked architecture and wood so is a carpenter and general handyman fixer. My other was interested in mental health and very good with people, so went into clinical mental health work. But he has to write his reports at home as an office environment would cause him too much distraction and he would not be efficient in his work. Neither of those would have been obvious choices but they are both middle-aged now and happy enough in their lives. Good days and bad days, ups and downs, but that is life. They are both excellent at finding novel ways of approaching problems and also dealing with crises.

There are all sorts of alternative ways to live a good life and when you have ADHD or other ND differences. It is important to explore that creatively, but as we are all also individuals there is no special recipe for answering this question, just to explore it and use some of that ADHD alternative thinking to power you through. But yes people with ADHD can have good productive lives in so many ways, it is just the system that makes us think we can't. Many do.

Further reading:

The Miracle of Mindfulness, Thich Nhat Hahn (and any other of Thay's books on practice)

Zen and the Brain, towards an understanding of meditation and consciousness, J.H. Austin, M.D. MIT Press, 1999.

Too Loud, Too Bright, Too Fast, Too Tight: What to Do If You Are Sensory Defensive in an Overstimulating World. By Sharon Heller, Ph.D.,

Causal models of attention-deficit/hyperactivity disorder: from common simple deficits to multiple developmental pathways. EJS Sonuga-Barke 2005. Biological psychiatry 57 (11), 1231–1238

Genetic relationship between five psychiatric disorders estimated from genome-wide SNPs. Cross-Disorder Group of the Psychiatric Genomics Consortium 2013. Nature genetics 45 (9), 984–994

The ecological validity of delay aversion and response inhibition as measures of impulsivity in AD/HD: a supplement to the NIMH multimodal treatment study of AD/HD. MV Solanto, H Abikoff, E Sonuga-Barke, R Schachar, GD Logan, T Wigal, … 2001 Journal of abnormal child psychology 29 (3), 215–228

ADDitude magazine for all things to do with ADHD

ADDers organisation also for all things ADHD

www.ingramcontent.com/pod-product-compliance
Lightning Source LLC
Chambersburg PA
CBHW060152050426
42446CB00013B/2779